CAPE HENLOPEN LIGHTHOUSE (1765-1926)

"For one hundred and eighty two years, the beacon known as Henlopen Lighthouse faced staunchly the lapping of the waves, the roll of the surf, the receding sands and the howling winds that wept across the shore of the Cape. Many thousands of shipmasters have watched with eagerness the light of that old tower, the glow of which guided them to a harbor of safety …

It might have been possible to save the Henlopen Light but the recent effort to protect it from falling was delayed too long. That old beacon, cared for by scores of men since its erection, is now to become simply one more memory for Delawareans to cherish, in that it was the second lighthouse to be built along the coast of what came to be known as the United States of America."

From An Account Written At The Time Of The Collapse

LIVING LEWES: AN INSIDER'S GUIDE
By Neil Shister

Design Director, Rob Waters

Mulberry Street Press
4711 Rodman Street, NW
Washington, DC 20016
www.MulberryStreetPress.com

Notice of Liability:
Reasonable care has been taken in the preparation of the text to ensure clarity and accuracy. The author and publisher disclaim any liability, loss or risk, personal or otherwise, which is incurred as a consequence, directly or indirectly, of the use and application of any of the contents of this book.

First Edition: July 4, 2013

ISBN: 978-0-9835969-2-9

Printed and Bound in the United States of America

TO ORDER COPIES www.LivingLewes.com

LIVING LEWES
An Insider's Guide

By Neil Shister

Rob Waters, Design Director

The Mulberry Street Collective
(Rob Sturgeon, Molly MacMillan,
Stephanie Bell, Cari Flowers)

Mulberry Street Press

TABLE OF CONTENTS

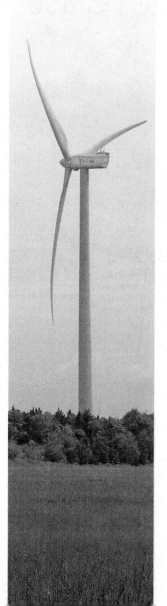

WE HAVE SOMETHING HERE THAT'S VALUABLE

Ted Becker was elected Mayor of Lewes in 2014, after ten years on the City Council, succeeding James Ford who had served for five terms until retiring. An occupational therapist by profession, Becker is a mid-west native (central Ohio) who was introduced to Lewes in 1978 and became a full time resident in 2000 when he acquired the Inn at Canal Square.

I Lewes has been well served by Mayor Ford and is on a firm foundation. In the last ten years, nearly $30 million of public and private funds have been invested in such things as the waste water treatment facility, rehabilitation and expansion of City Hall, Second Street, Bay Ave., Madison and Railroad Avenues rehabilitation Projects, and the Canalfront Park. We're in good shape.

This community has really come a long way in a relatively short period. The intellectual capital here is amazing; but there are still ever-changing needs. In the last census our full-time residents went from 3000 to 2700. In-season we more than double in population.

We are surrounded by water or marshland on three sides, which pushes the majority of development in one direction; west. Any large commercial or residential project that might be developed along these roads could severely impact accessibility to Lewes. We must work with county officials and developers to insure we remain accessible.

Development is always a central concern. We're hiring a city planner for the first time, on a consultant basis, to help us better respond to pressures for development and look at the broader picture. It's always a matter of balance. Rather than be reactionary, we need to be proactive in our planning efforts.

The new 28,000 square foot library on Kings Highway with the adjacent bicycle path trailhead to Georgetown, Lewes Rails and Trails with access to the Junction Breakwater and Gordon's Pont Trails, are our major current opportunities. The library is a $10.5 million project designed as a gathering place for the community and will have a tremendous impact on Lewes for the next fifty years. I see it as the 'next' Canalfront Park. We anticipate construction of the Library and Trailhead to begin early in 2016.

Better connectivity with our neighbors is also a good way to improve the quality of life. There's a conversation underway about further developing the canal water taxi service to provide a docking point in Rehoboth.

Community resiliency in the wake of climate change is a major issue that we are working to address. Lewes must start preparing for whatever is coming in the way of sea level rise, coastal surges, and global warming. The primary impact of climate change would be felt on the beach side; the town side of the canal is mostly on higher ground however areas toward the University are more likely to be impacted.

Lewes is an extraordinary place,. Everyone who comes here has so many opportunities to get involved, from Fort Miles and the Overfalls Lightship to Coastal Concerts or the Friends of the Cape Henlopen State Park. What is even more extraordinary is the degree of both physical and financial support and the involvement our residents and visitors have in these many worthwhile and interesting endeavors. ■

LEWES CORE VALUES

During the 1990s, a long-range planning commission was convened to produce a civic vision to lead Lewes for the next fifty years. Numerous public meetings were held to solicit citizen opinion. From these conversations came a set of community core values that continue to guide the Council.

Core Value #1: Lewes has a special and historic relationship with the sea.
Core Value #2: Lewes is a community of diversity.
Core Value #3: Lewes values its human town scale and sense of face-to-face intimacy that is characteristic of its quality of life.
Core Value #4: Lewes is a town of busy days and quiet nights.
Core Value #5: Lewes recognizes and maintains its internal communities.
Core Value #6: Lewes has a unique historical origin and strives to highlight its heritage through building design and architectural preservation.

INTRODUCTING LEWES
A TALE OF DISCOVERY

Wilma is a spunky woman of indeterminate age, face deeply bronzed, not local-born but a Lewes resident since 1982. She moved from suburban Washington because she wanted to live by the water ("which I've done!"). On Thursdays she works the cash register at the Historical Society shop on Second Street, next to the labyrinth etched in the grass adjoining the St. Peter's cemetery. It is a low-ceilinged building beamed with shipwreck timber that dates from the 1620s, perhaps the oldest structure in America sitting on its original foundation.

When asked what she likes about Lewes, Wilma chooses her words carefully. "Everyone here feels protective," she says after a pause. "We know what a special place it is. We treasure its uniqueness."

The uniqueness of Lewes begins with the name itself which, contrary to spelling and natural inclination, is pronounced "Loo-iss" rather than "Lew-zzz."

The name dates from 1682, as the dispute between Maryland and Pennsylvania over the three "lower counties" bordering what was then known as the "South River" was tilting in William Penn's favor. That year, on the occasion of Penn's first visit to America, the settlement at the mouth of the Delaware Bay was re-named in honor of the English market town of his youth (when young William lost his hair from the pox as a boy, the family moved from London to their country mansion in Sussex to spare him embarrassment).

Swanendael, 'valley of the swans,' was what the first Europeans called this place, dazzled by flocks of black-billed tundra swan wintering along the swampy wetlands (the creek would be widened three hundred years later into the Lewes-Rehoboth Canal). These were Dutchmen, following in the wake of Henry Hudson's search for a Northwest Passage to China.

Twenty-eight men arrived in 1631, settling on a strip of land eight miles long acquired from the native Algonquin for cloth and beads. They raised a palisade stake fence around a cookhouse and communal dormitory, intent on pursuing their charter from the Dutch West India Company "to carry out the whale fishery in that region, and to plant a colony for the cultivation of all sorts of grain, for which the country is very well suited and of tobacco."

Eighteen months later, two ships arrived from Holland to find only charred ruins. The original inhabitants had been massacred by the natives, victims of a convoluted tale of insulted honor and revenge. A later wave of settlers, throwing caution to the wind, chose to stay anyway.

Such is the determined stock from which Lewes stems, many of whose descendants lay buried in the town's several graveyards under mossy tombstones etched with still faintly visible dates from the 1600s and 1700s.

For much of its life, Lewes' allure was mostly that of a hardscrabble survivor. The seat of Sussex County moved fifteen miles west to Georgetown in 1791 and with it went the town's rank (although it would produce four state Governors). In the War of 1812, the British blockaded the harbor; after the locals refused to provide supplies, they bombarded the town (a cannonball can be seen embedded in the 'Cannonball House' along Front Street). The moments worth marking with civic pride over the ensuing years were largely unexceptional: the building of a lighthouse, the arrival of the railroad, a first class of graduates from the Union School.

Throughout the middle years of the 20th century, a perpetual stink hovered in the air, the smell of tons of sardine-like menhaden being pressed into oils and fertilizer (in 1938 the Consolidated Fisheries Company of Lewes was the biggest processing plant in the United States). For several decades, Lewes ranked among the largest landing ports in the country (a home base fleet of 25 ships employed over 600 crew members). But by the 1950s, the waters were fished out and shipbuilding had long since disappeared.

Perhaps just as much as history, setting accounts for Lewes' spirit of place. The beachscape

here is unlike any other along this stretch of coast, run-off from the Appalachians geological eons ago, back filling the Bay. The prevailing south-to-north currents, unusual along this stretch of the Atlantic, would whittle out Cape Henlopen, and create in the Great Dune (atop of which the guns of Fort Miles peered out during World War II) the highest waterfront point between Cape Cod and Cape Hatteras.

It would be geography that prompted the 'renaissance' of Lewes. For want of a precise moment, more than a few folks date the re-birth of Lewes to when King's Ice Cream opened in 1981, providing a reason to come to town after dark.

Local citizens, their sense of pride reinvigorated, began restoring the town's extraordinary housing stock and buildings that mirror the time-line of the nation. Visitors, perhaps wearied from the atmosphere in other beach towns, began to 'find' this oasis of timelessness, so different in tone and character from its neighbors.

Going on four centuries now, Lewes has sustained and built upon its distinctive character. Staying alive, as those original colonizers discovered, could never be taken for granted. One survives by one's wits and talents here. A living earned from the sea or the fields or the tourists has to be re-claimed every season. It doesn't breed fast money. But it does nurture an enduring spirit, a communal mystique, that---as Wilma at the Historical Society shop rightly notes---makes it special.

Those who come to love Lewes---be it for a brief visit or an extended stay--- almost always have a tale of discovery to share, of how they unexpectedly happened upon this unlikely historic town at the cape where the Delaware meets the Atlantic. And of that moment of personal recognition when they intuitively understood, without having to be told, "to treasure its uniqueness." ■

By Neil Shister

CANALFRONT PARK
THE TOWN BACKYARD

Canalfront Park, three open-space acres of terraces, paths and playgrounds in the center of town alongside the Lewes-Rehoboth Canal, has been rightly called a 'shining jewel' of recent American public landscapes.

This setting, regarded as Lewes' collective backyard (complete with playground, boat slips and kayak put-in), has been the heart of the community for almost four centuries.

During the Revolutionary War, patriots kept their watercraft secured here to deny supplies to the British. A toll bridge once led across the canal to the marshy grasslands for grazing livestock, picking berries, and harvesting oysters. Boat-building flourished well into the 19th cen-

tury in this spot, launching craft at a landing near where the Lightship Overfalls now anchors. Canalfront Park is a celebration of a rich maritime past.

But it is much more than an historical marker. It is alive and vibrant, a tribute to the dedication of local citizens who mobilized in 1999 to purchase what had become the barren remnants of the Lewes Boatyard and Marina. The grounds were littered with two industrial wenches, a concrete block house and heavy nets more than a thousand feet in diameter that had been used until the waters were fished out.

The site was destined to become condos and stores, a commercial development of such size

that it would dwarf its surroundings and permanently block off the water view. The project was well in play, on the verge of receiving zoning permission. Until members of the community, initially mobilized by Joe Stewart, came forth with an alternative vision: a beautifully landscaped common space that would reconnect the historic town core to the ever-changing waterfront.

Some 15 years later, that original vision is now reality.

Today Canalfront Park ranks as the heart of Lewes. Toddlers slide and swing on an inventive playscape. Families picnic on the lush 'Village Green'. Strollers amble along promenades landscaped with native plantings. There is a dock to fish. On summer evenings, concerts take place. Movies are shown. A free yoga class has become a Sunday morning tradition. ■

FRIENDS OF THE PARK

Canalfront is sustained through community support. It is important to the life of Lewes and there are ambitious plans to make it even more important in the future. If you love downtown Lewes and care about its future, please consider becoming a Friend of the Park. You can make a contribution at www.lewescanalfrontpark.org/support .

An Endowment Fund with a goal of $1.5 million is also being created to support the Park in perpetuity. To learn more about the three-year pledge plan or make a bequest, contact: Friends of the Lewes Canalfront Park, PO Box 110, Lewes DE 19958.

THE MAKING OF CANALFRONT PARK

Joseph Stewart is the former Chair of the Greater Lewes Foundation.

In 1997, the land was sitting there---an old boatyard, a Quonset hut, lots of junk scattered around. It was a dump. The asking price was $1.5 million. Several developers were about to buy it and nobody really cared until we saw what was planned. It was going to be a large residential-commercial project, over-scaled for the site and for the surrounding community. The entire water view would be blocked. There was going to be a substantial number of boat slips.

Once I started working on the park, I got a new appreciation for the waterfront and what it means to Lewes. It's an iconic location and once it's lost, it would be lost forever.

I always thought this was a one-time chance to save this amount of land. I didn't own the Inn at Canal Square at that point, so there was no hidden agenda on my part.

We tried to get city officials to stop it. Mayor George Smith was supportive, he said he'd help if we got traction. But the real message was less hopeful, 'if they meet the zoning requirements, there's nothing we can do.'

Ten people started meeting at my home once a week for two years, strategizing and organizing. There is an amazing depth and breadth of talent in this city that you can tap into. And it's a generous city. Over ten years, we raised $11 million to challenge the zoning, purchase the land, plan a park, and finally install a park. All this was done with citizen involvement every step of the way. We posted signs all over the city: 'Would you like to see a park instead of a condo?'

It was still the 'old boy' system back then, this was the first time anybody had really tried to resist. And there was a lot of money to be made from this project. We needed fire-power to mount a credible opposition. We had to hire lawyers, traffic engineers, environmental consultants, people to review every aspect of their plan.

At a big meeting, where the hall was packed, we had primed one of the Council members to ask the developers' about their plan for the waterfront. 'Nothing definite yet,' they answered, 'we'll leave it pretty much pristine.' But we had already obtained a copy of their permit from the Corps of Engineers requesting a large number of boat slips and confronted them with it. That was a defining moment. Their side went downhill from then. All of a sudden, the politicians started getting interested.

We hired a firm out of Washington, The Waterfront Center, to help develop our approach to a park. Hundreds of people participated, the process lasted a year. The community's priorities were that the park have a maritime theme, that it not be 'boutique-y', that it be sustainable, and that it be attractive to all age groups.

At this point we formed the Greater Lewes Foundation to help the city chase grants. We set out to raise money locally, from state sources, federal sources. Everywhere. One weekend we sent out volunteers to get 100 people to each pledge $1000. They got them and each of those pledges was redeemed.

The price of the land had by then gone up to $2 million. That seemed like a fortune but Dave Burton, an early supporter of the park, said 'whatever you pay for it now, you'll think it was the bargain of the century in ten years.' He was right. Today as raw land the park's worth between $12 million and $15 million.

The city owned a parcel of land adjacent to Cape Henlopen Park that the state wanted. The city sold it for $500,000 and dedicated the money to the acquisition of the park. Now everybody wanted to be a part of it.

Bill Clinton was President, and Mrs. Clinton had gotten behind a program called "Save America's Treasures" in the Interior Department. The Mayor and a few members of the Foundation went to Washington to make a pitch for an earmark. In a previous life, I used to be the Staff Counsel for Interior on the Senate Appropriation Committee, I represented our efforts pro bono. What ensued was straight out of 'Perils of Pauline' but, at the final moment in the last wrap-up on the floor, we got $2 million. That let us go ahead. We bought the land in 2002.

The Foundation spent the next eight years raising money. We even got one of the original developers who wanted to build the commercial project to give us the proceeds from one of his lots, worth $30,000.

The next big step was developing a master plan and design. The firm the Council hired, Andropogon of Philadelphia, produced a very contemporary approach. Nothing 'cutesy-wutesy.' The benches are like Mies van der Rohe designs. The shade arbor is held up with stainless steel cable so it is reminiscent of a ship. There are rain gardens in the park to help with sustainability so water doesn't flow directly into the Canal. All the plantings are indigenous. We put in around forty boat slips including some for itinerants because people go from Maine to Florida in their boats but they never used to stop in Lewes.

In 2010 we had the formal dedication of the park. We showed people what can be done when the community comes together in the common good. You just need to get out there and work and see what happens. ∎

WHERE THE OCEAN MEETS THE BAY

The discovery of Lewes begins with the sea and the shore. The first explorers arrived looking for a water passage to the Orient, today's visitors are still drawn by the ocean. The singular ecology nurtured by this setting is the foundation for all that follows.

THE MIDDLE BIGHT

Standing on the Great Dune in Cape Henlopen State Park looking to the Atlantic, it's hard to imagine that what you're seeing would have all been Arctic tundra some 17,000 years ago as the Ice Age began to end. The shoreline would be some 75 miles further east at the edge of what is now the Continental Shelf.

Huge glaciers covered New York, New Jersey, and Northern Pennsylvania known as the Laurentide Ice Sheets. When the climate warmed and the ice melted, the hard rock of the Piedmont washed down, leaving deposits along the way as the sea level rose to make the coastline we now know.

Today you are standing on a ten thousand-foot thick slab of those soft sediments that we call the state of Delaware. It is gradually subsiding under its own weight. Powerful wave actions over eons have created the sandy beach, the shoreline etched and eroded by steady south-to-north currents.

As a consequence of its geological dynamics, Delaware has the lowest sea level elevation of the 50 states. This glacial outwash has brought more dinosaur fossils to Delaware than anywhere else in the eastern United States (the indigenous local Lenape tribe told a myth about a great monster so terrifying that it left footprints in the rocks, a reference now thought to be fossilized Tyrannosaurus Rex tracks).

The glacial runoff also produced several broad channels which backfilled with ocean water, known geologically as 'drowned river valleys.' The Delaware Bay is the prime example, a sea-level valley which gradually became submerged (its average depth is slightly more than thirty feet). The inland bays at Rehoboth and Dewey, by contrast, are shallow coastal lagoons behind a narrow barrier island.

The defining feature of the Delaware Bay is that it is an estuary, the mouth of a large river where the tide meets the stream. Salinity, the salt density caused by the mix of ocean with fresh water, is its controlling ecological factor, affecting the aquatic and wetland habitats, and the species that live in these habitats.

The largest and arguably the most important tributary along the estuary's 133 miles is the Schuylkill River, emptying into the Port of Philadelphia and providing nearly 10% of the freshwater. The Christina River Basin, another important tributary system, enters at Wilmington. The Delaware basin is one of the most heavily industrialized watersheds in the country, from the anthracite coal industry of the lower Lehigh Valley and the stretch from Trenton to Philadelphia with extensive production of chemicals, metals, textiles and paper.

The tidal area of the Bay is among the most fertile stretches along the northern Atlantic coast for the propagation and growth of marine organisms. Numerous species of floating life (plankton), swimming life (nekton), and bottom life (benthon) are found throughout the estuary. Saltwater fish in their northern migration are attracted to feed on these organisms. The shallow waters of the Bay and coastal area off Cape Henlopen is an ideal spawning ground, the small fish feeding on minute crustacean and algae and themselves becoming prey for larger fish and crabs.

From your spot atop the Great Dune, you are staring at what is thought to be the second youngest of the five oceans. The Atlantic did not exist until the ancestral super-continent Pangaea broke up 130 million years ago and then started drifting apart. The expanse of sea you are surveying is known to mariners as 'the Middle Bight' (a bight being the bend in a rope between two points). Stretching from Nantucket Shoals to North Carolina, this body of water contains two ocean currents; the warmer Gulf Stream 200 miles offshore slips past an offshoot of the colder Labrador current bringing over 300 migrating species of fish into the area.

Think of the New Jersey Turnpike with schools of fish in the North and Southbound lanes each looking for the Delaware Bay exit. From the north, large schools of Weakfish, Shad, and Striped bass swim into Delaware Bay in the spring to spawn while from the south, the Lizardfish, Sheepshead, and increasing numbers of Florida Pompano are using the Bay for food and rest. As their names suggest, Winter Flounder (with their dorsal eye on the right side looking from tail-to-head) arrive in winter and Summer Flounder (eye on the left) in summer.

Most of these fish are temporary visitors, typically arriving or leaving the Bay when the water temperature hovers around 55 degrees. There are, however, several species that stay year round, like the Mummichugs, Bay Anchovies, Yellow Perch, and Longmouth Bass.

Seabirds fly skyward as you stare out from your perch atop the Great Dune. They are themselves following the ocean migration.

If your timing is right (following a full moon in May or June), you might spot a Redknot (a largish sandpiper) in migration from the tip of South America to their Arctic nesting ground. You are seeing them as they just complete the leg of their flight from the north coast of Brazil to Delaware Bay, some 3000 miles, which they traverse in a mere three or four days. They have landed to feast on the newly laid eggs of Horseshoe Crabs that have come to shore en masse (Lewes Bay is one of the specie's primary breeding grounds). The Redknots arrive in dire straits, having lost one-third of their body weight en route. The soft, easily digested eggs are the perfect food because the bird had shrunk its stomach prior to its journey to accommodate the enlarged heart and lungs required to make the flight.

A host of competing shorebirds also favor the sandy shores of the lower Bay. Keep your eyes peeled for Brown Pelicans, Osprey, even an occasional Bald Eagle. Sanderlings can be seen scurrying between successive waves, swifter runners than other shorebirds because they have no back toe on their feet. The most common gull is the Ring-billed (a black band circles its yellow bill), sociable birds known for performing acrobatic tricks in mid-air.

In the marshes and mudflats of the inland estuaries, Dunlins, Dowithchers, and the Semi-Palmated Sandpiper dig for food. The tidal flats and creeks are home to the long-legged wading birds. The Glossy Ibis, with it's curving bill, and the Blue Heron, which fly with their necks retracted, are usually found in mating pairs in the marsh grasses.

The interplay of warm and cold waters converging off Lewes is mirrored in the climate dynamics that shape the local weather. The prevailing Westerly winds bring Arctic air masses to this region in the winter and warm Gulf air masses in the summer which generate powerful storms. Hurricane season runs from the beginning of June through the end of November, although it is not unheard of for them to occur at other times. Nor'easters can be accompanied by hurricane force winds and cause severe coastal flooding and erosion.

This extraordinary natural world, where the ocean meets the bay, is a powerful teacher. As you look out, you are witnessing a fragile yet resilient web that sustains a complex chain of life. ∎

By Rob Sturgeon

INSIDER'S GUIDE TO THE BEACHES

LEWES BEACH

A half-mile or so from the center of town, where Savannah Road dead-ends just past the Dairy Queen, lies the Lewes public beach. The usually calm surf and warmer water of the Bay here make for an especially 'user-friendly' venue for families with small children and those interested in a restful setting. Here you'll find free parking, public restrooms, lifeguards, benches and white sand.

To the left, either by foot or along Cedar Street by bicycle or car, is a wide expanse of continuing Bay beach stretching to Roosevelt Inlet. On the other side of the dunes are residential homes including many summer rentals. Much sailing, kayaking, and swimming occurs along this stretch. This area is unguarded without public restrooms.

At the end of the sandy beach if you are walking, or the free gravel parking lot at the end of Cedar Street if you are biking or driving, is an area the locals call Fisherman's Beach because of the massive stone break-wall that makes it a good spot to catch the many varieties of Delaware Bay's finest seafood.

BEACH #2

Heading east in the other direction from Lewes beach along Henlopen Drive at Georgia Drive, is the entrance to "Beach #2". This beach is rarely crowded although considered an ideal spot for wind surfers, paddle-boarders, and kayakers. It is also a great place to view the ferry coming in from Cape May and, when it's in port, the tall ship Kalmar Nyckel.

CAPE HENLOPEN STATE PARK

Past the ferry terminal lays the entrance to Cape Henlopen State Park, with its wide variety of beaches for different tastes ($4 per day for Delaware residents, $8 per day out-of-state). Ask for a map at the park entrance gate with directions to the beaches.

The Fishing Pier, a quarter-mile wooden walkway into the surf, provides an informal trail-head to both bay and ocean beaches. The Pier itself is open 24-hours a day and affords a superb vantage point for ocean gazing as well as fishing (a well-equipped bait shop is off the parking lot). To the left of the Pier is the last Bay beach, to the right an unguarded ocean beach that curves to Cape Henlopen point (from March through October parts of this area are restricted to protect the breeding nests of endangered migratory seabirds).

North Beach (commonly referred to as 'Bathhouse Beach' because its big public changing room and showers) is the largest beach, straight out of central casting for those seeking a classic 'ole timey' family frolic by the sea. This is the park's 'beach central' with abundant parking, bare-boned but welcome food concessions, a boardwalk down to the water and life guard stations every few hundred yards. To the south, the great mound of forested sand covers the batteries of Fort Miles and the Great Dune. Compared to the Jersey Shore, North Beach is still quaint and rustic, the simplicity makes for great charm.

Herring Point offers the most rugged beach experience. The small parking lot has a panoramic view out to sea, the walk down to the water is easy to navigate but just steep enough to make little kids feel daring. There are no lifeguards or services here but usually plenty of boogie-boarders. This is where surfers hang out, alongside a stone beakwall. Locals are especially fond of Herring Point, they come here when they want to savor the scene in solitude. One can walk from here all the way to Rehoboth.

Point Comfort Station, on the opposite side of North Beach from Herring Point, affords a crossover where four wheel-drive vehicles that are properly licensed for surf fishing can drive on the sand (permits can be obtained at the park office, $65 per year for Delaware residents, $130 for non-residents) . Don't try to sneak on, the fine for driving illegally on the sand is steep. There is also a hefty fine should you get stuck and have to be towed. Savvy locals know to deflate their tires in advance and re-inflate them afterwards at the air hoses set up by the side of the road. Beachers come here as well as fisher-folk, the strip is less populated than the more crowded North Beach although one has to be alert to avoid fishing lines cast in the waves.

A bit past Point Comfort is a scenic overlook from which one can gaze out past the bird reserve to the tip of the point. A slightly sloping descent at the end of the parking lot leads to a beach favored by locals for picnic suppers. Looking westward, this spot affords great views of the sunset behind the nearby lighthouse, which are simply spectacular. ∎

WE LOVE THE BEACHES AND HAVE TAKEN GREAT ADVANTAGE OF THEM OVER THE YEARS

There is nothing like body surfing at Cape Henlopen, catching a wave and having its power take you like a plank right up onto the sand. It's pure exhilaration. Just you and the wave.

Surf fishing is terrific. Fall is the best time but spring can be great when the trout run starts. Local folks go fishing right on Lewes Beach, they know the spots where the water gets warm earliest and where the sea trout come in. I also have great summer memories of casting in toward the East End Lighthouse on the Delaware breakwater, and catching beautiful flounder.

One of the things we used to do that was a lot of fun— although you aren't allowed anymore— was 'seining'. Seining is where you go out into the surf with a big net, trap whatever is in the water and drag it to the beach to see what shows up. We commissioned a 150-foot long net with two big wooden dowels on either end and would take that haul-seine out with a crew of kids and friends, then haul it up to the beach. It was like a great treasure hunt. There would be stripers, horseshoe crabs, conch shells or whelks with live conch in them, blue crabs, eels, croakers, even dogfish sharks. Everybody would come a-running to discover what was in the net.

Of course, the beach is also a great place to run, to walk, to go watch the sunrise or sunset. Just to get away from the cares of the world. This is very important to the people who live here.

Because we're on the edge of the continent, the beach is also a place of great activity. It is very dynamic. Every four or five years, for example, there is a winter storm and whole rows of star fish get thrown up onto the beach or witches purses or necklaces of conch shells. You never know what you'll find. Once in a while, there's leftover mortar casting remnants from Fort Miles.

Of all the sustained pleasure that I've had on the beach, I think beachcombing has been the most fun— especially after storms. You can go out to the point right now and find remnants of shipwrecks. One winter, I found one of those big timbers with spikes in them and it got me to thinking about the Blizzard of 1888 when 75 ships were destroyed— that timber might have been from one of those ships. I've even found bottles out there with messages in them, people will take the ferry and put messages in a bottle and throw them overboard.

Another time, the dredge digging up sand off the Yacht Club a half-mile offshore from Lewes Beach ran into an 18th century shipwreck. Artifacts were spewing all along the beach. People were picking up bottles, glass, toy soldiers, all kinds of stuff.

As an 'insider,' my words of advice to visitors would be to fully experience the beaches of Lewes as a rare space that is the meeting point between two great ecosystems, the ocean and the continent. ■

DOGFISH SHARK

The Smooth Dogfish Shark, namesake and logo for the fabled local brewery, is the most abundant shark found in the Bay. They migrate here in late spring, when the water temperature reaches 55-60 degrees, and birth ten to twenty pups. They feed on lobsters, crabs, clams, and small fish by crushing and grinding the hard shells with their flat teeth. The Smooth Dogfish, usually brown or gray, can change color from dark to light to avoid predators. As the waters cool, they head south to inhabit the continental shelf and inland bays as deep as 200 feet.

Adults can reach a length of 3-4 feet, weigh 20 pounds, and are commonly reeled in (and put back) by surf fishermen. Local palates, however, are beginning to acquire a taste for dogfish. They are also used for research into eye transplants, nervous systems, and pharmaceuticals.

WHELK

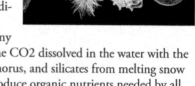

Whelk is a generic name for various kinds of sea snails commonly seen along the Delaware shore. Their ornate shells are recognizable by concentric whorls arranged in a clockwise pattern. The snails inside can live as long as forty years. They are predatory, acting like a vacuum cleaner that sucks up dead or weakened animals from the sea floor. Some secrete a chemical that dissolves the calcium in sea shells allowing them to ingest clams and crabs. Whelks are quite a hardy species, having survived the Great Extinction 250 million years ago when 99% of the planet's species disappeared.

PLANKTON

Phylopankton, too tiny to see, are the foundation of the food chain that makes the Bay such a uniquely rich, diverse feeding ground. These tiny algae combine the CO_2 dissolved in the water with the nitrogen, phosphorus, and silicates from melting snow and runoff to produce organic nutrients needed by all life in the estuary. As a by-product, they give off oxygen.

The most common of the hundreds of varieties is the diatom, which likes the colder spring time waters and creates a minor bloom which supports the oyster larvae and weakfish in their growth cycle. As the water warms, a brown algae becomes dominant which feeds the fish and shellfish stock. A lurking danger is the potentially destructive red algae that release toxic chemicals, although they are typically kept in check by the strong tidal mixing and relatively low light levels in the Delaware estuary.

HORSESHOE CRAB

Horseshoe Crabs are one of the planet's oldest species, perhaps 250 million years old. These ancient crustaceans swim upside-down along the ocean floor looking for worms and small mollusks, and are more closely related to spiders than the crabs we eat today. They are hardy, able to survive a year without food and withstand wide ranges of temperature allowing them to live in the cold Mid- Atlantic and also to migrate into the warm shallow waters of Delaware Bay to spawn.

An extraordinary sight, on the night of the New or Full moon in May or June, are thousands of breeding packs (multiple males to each female) swarming the beaches to lay and fertilize their eggs. Lewes is one of the great spots where this happens. In hot pursuit later will come the Red Knot, a plump sandpiper that might well be the world's long-distance flying champion. It migrates each year from Tierra del Fuego at the tip of South America to the northern Arctic Tundra, stopping in Lewes to re-fuel on the nutritionally rich Horseshoe Crab eggs.

STRIPED BASS

The Striped Bass or Rockfish is the major sport fish caught by boats sailing out of Lewes harbor. It has been hooked in the ocean, off the Delaware Bay and in tidewater tributaries. A good fighter when caught on a line, the fish can grow as long as 4 ½ feet, weigh up to 80 pounds, and live for 30 years.

The mature adult is easily identified by several dark horizontal stripes along it's silvery sides. It spawns in the fresh water of the Delaware River, and upper Chesapeake Bay. The young spend their first summer in shallow low-salinity shore areas and tidal creeks. In their second summer, they are ready for the Bay and by winter they will swim into the open ocean until they return in the spring, completing the cycle. In 1982 there were only an estimated five million Striped Bass due to overfishing, but with strict licensing and management the stock has recovered today to 56 million.

PIPING PLOVER

The northern tip of Cape Henlopen beach is off-limits to visitors from March to October, protected by a fence to provide undisturbed habitat in the dunes for the endangered Piping Plover to breed. Males court by digging out nests near the grass line, females choose the one they like best and proceed to decorate it with shells and debris for camouflage. The original census in 1987 found two breeding pairs here; the estimate now is approximately one dozen.

THE STATE OF THE BAY
'MUCH PROGRESS HAS BEEN MADE IMPROVING THE BAY HABITAT'

Roy Miller, Policy Coordinator for the Center for the Inland Bays, has four decades experience as a Fisheries Biologist for Delaware Fish and Wildlife Services.

The timing of the Delaware Coastal Zone Act in 1971, which prohibited new heavy industry outside the Port of Wilmington, couldn't have been better because a major oil refinery was in the planning stages and this Act put a stop to its development. The Act also blocked the development of offshore bulk product transfer facilities in the middle of Delaware Bay that posed the added threat of oil spills and leakages.

The second major impact on Bay water quality was the amendment to the Federal Clean Water Act of 1972 that provided funding for sewage treatment facilities. The lower Delaware River received five new plants able to handle the bulk of raw sewage that was discharging into the river. In the following years, the water quality dramatically improved to the extent that the 30 mile 'Dead Zone' or pollution block in the upper bay, which had prohibited native fish species from migrating to their spawning ground, disappeared. American Shad and Striped Bass have reappeared.

The level of industrial pollutants in the Bay has decreased significantly, but there are still periodic advisories on consuming fish from the Bay. Rutgers University has developed disease resistant strains of oysters that are being used to restart the industry in the middle bay where the salinity is more favorable for their survival.

The whole tidal wetland area is undergoing significant change with the gradual increase in the sea level along the shoreline. Delaware Department of Natural Resources projects a sea level rise of 20 – 57 inches over the next century. The fate of tidal wetlands will be determined by competition with commercial and housing development as they all migrate inland away from the rising seas." ∎

Cape May-Lewes Ferry

'Take a Break from the Ordinary'

If you've got a taste for light adventure, the most exciting way to reach Lewes is aboard the Lewes-Cape May (New Jersey) Ferry.

The 17-mile crossing is just exotic enough to be romantic. The trip takes 85 minutes in calm seas, a perfect length of time. Dolphin sightings are common. Fare in-season is $44 one-way per car (passengers included), $10 for foot passengers. The fleet of ships runs all year and makes the crossing on a regular basis (check the current schedule at www.capemaylewes-ferry.com, 1-800-643-3779).

New luxury seating was installed on all ships in 2011, increasing the capacity in the salons by some 50% to over 300 passengers. The Bloody Mary's served on board have a loyal following ("seriously impressive," says one Yelp reviewer), food has been recently outsourced to Matt Haley's SoDel Concepts restaurant operation. There's arcade games for children.

The Lewes terminal is modern and welcoming, with free miniature golf and terrific crab bisque at a bargain price (it always runs out!). Savvy locals seeking a hamburger accompanied by a great vista of the Bay hang out at the On the Rocks Bar & Grill outside the terminal.

Two Lewes lighthouses are visible from the ferry. The 76-foot-tall white column is the Harbor of Refuge Lighthouse. Finished in 1926, it has a range of 19 miles and guards the "shears" or sandy shoals that form at the entrance to the harbor. The smaller 56-foot-lighthouse, which is red and brown, is called the East End Breakwater Light and was built earlier in 1885. No longer needed, its light was discontinued in 1996.

Instruments on board the ferry M/V Twin Capes measure various parameters of seawater at the mouth of Delaware Bay during its back-and-forth from Lewes to Cape May. Levels of salinity, pH, dissolved oxygen, chlorophyll, temperature and turbidity (cloudiness) are used as indicators for the quality-of-life in bay waters.

A word to the wise, the 100-car capacity often sells out in-season so reserve in advance. There's a shuttle bus through town to free off-site parking lots. For foot passengers coming over from Cape May, a bike rental awaits right at the Lewes terminal. ∎

LEWES History

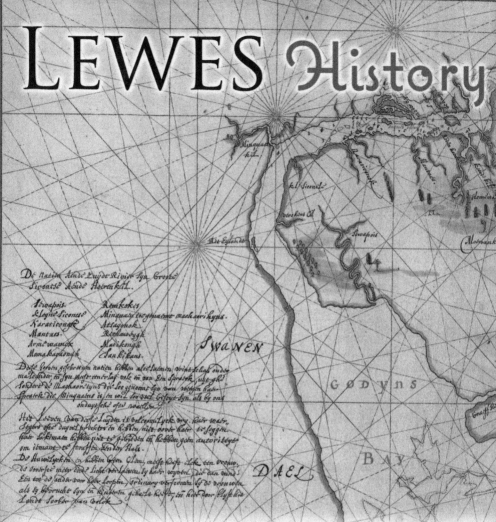

Translation:

The nations at the South Rver are Great Sironese at the Hoerenkil, Sewapois, Remkokes. Small Sironese, Minquaen (also named Machaorikyns), Naraticonck, Atsayonck, Mantaes, Rechaweygh, Armewamix, Matikongh, Momakavaongk, Sankikans.

These above described nations have friendships with each other. And are mostly one people with one language ... The life of these people is totally free. Their soothsayers or devil preachers have nothing to say over them, their shamans can't order them and have no authority to give someone a death penalty.

The marriages are not fixed, most have one wife, the chief more than one. And they leave their women easily, and these will go from one to another like a whore, usually women are disowned after having a child and as a result the population remains low.

NAUTICAL CHART
OF ZWAANENDAEL, 1639

Caerte vande
SVYDT RIVIER
in Niew·nederland.

Photo provided by Lewes historical Society

The Duke of Windsor visits Beebe Hospital in 1940, flanked by the brothers Beebe.

LEWES SAW THE WORLD GO BY ITS DOOR

I first came to Lewes when I was four or five, my parents were teachers who brought the family here every summer from Cleveland because it was the nearest Atlantic coast beach. The town felt 'ancient' to a kid, a magical place where you could step back in time.

What makes Lewes so special is that so much that mattered happened here.

The port was the entry point to the Bay that led to Philadelphia, which was the political and commercial capital of America in the 1700s. That meant that Lewes saw the world go by its doors. The Chesapeake has access to the Atlantic but it faces inward, its perspective is insular. The Delaware Bay, on the other hand, looks out. It's the only significant body of water between New York and Norfolk where ships can pull in to shelter from a storm. Lewes was known as 'the harbor of refuge.'

The influences on Lewes were cosmopolitan.

People came here from all over the world. Some were shipwrecked, others awaiting orders until their next voyage. All kinds of people lived in Lewes--- Europeans, Asians, you name it. The pilots going out to bring in the foreign ships were exposed to international influences, too. There was no other place like it on the Delmarva coast.

Even though Lewes was a fairly remote town, fashion and style worked their way down in a way that didn't happen anywhere else along the Peninsula. Take the Burton-Ingram House on the grounds of the Historical Society, for example. Its stairwell is open through three floors, the equal on a smaller scale to the grand floating staircase of Winterthur. There are things all over Lewes that you'd never expect to find in a small town like this.

The ship channel to Philadelphia is on our side of the bay, a mile or two off the Delaware side. The New Jersey side is too shallow. So Lewes' importance in defending the Bay has always been a mili-

5797   SECOND STREET, LEWES, DEL.   ILLUSTRATED POST CARD CO., N. Y.

Dr Hiram Burton Home

Photo provided by Lewes historical Society

tary priority. In the Revolutionary War, the fort was called the Upper Fort and located where the cannons are by the town dock near the Draw Bridge. It protected the DuPont gun powder mills in Wilmington, at that time a new industry that was supplying George Washington's army. The reason the British had to march on Philadelphia via the Chesapeake was that they couldn't get past Lewes up the Delaware.

The inner breakwater at the East End lighthouse was one of the engineering marvels of the world when it was started in 1830. This was the biggest infrastructure project the U.S. had ever undertaken. Lewes had the second longest seawall in the world when it was finally finished after the Civil War, comparable to the great ports of Plymouth, England and Cherbourg, France.

Fort Miles, in what is now Cape Henlopen State Park, was built in 1941 with massive 155 mm 6-inch guns that had a three mile range to fend off German U-boats. They were a threat to the oil refineries outside Philadelphia. Throughout World War II, German submarines were just off-shore. The media embargoed the news from the public, so nobody knew.

If I had to tell visitors 'the one thing to see,' I guess I'd say 'don't miss Mulberry Street.' I don't know any other street like it in America, three blocks where you can find houses dating from every century starting in the 1700's up to today.

Mulberry used to be called Knitting Street because old women would be sitting on their porch knitting. At one end, at the corner of Second,

you've got the oldest house in Delaware. Up the street, there's an example of what John Wesley, the founder of Methodism, called a 'one room preaching house,' the Methodist Meeting House built in 1790 (now a private home). Lewes is the birthplace of Methodism in the U.S. Between Third and Fourth Streets is a block of Victorian homes in a style called 'handyman Gothics' with decorative gingerbread porches. No two are alike. The former Bethel Methodist Chapel, a magnificent building now converted into condos, is further up the block at the corner of Church Street.

It's just a treat to walk down Mulberry Street. There's very few places in America where you can stroll several blocks and see houses that date from the beginning to the end of our nation's history. So if you're eating ice cream one evening at King's, take a stroll down Mulberry Street—it's two minutes away, intersecting Second Street past the graveyard.

The way I'd sum up Lewes is that this is a real town with a real history and a real present. It's not just a beach town. For hundreds of years, Lewes has been here. Early guidebooks about historic places to visit in the United States always included Lewes. The famous painter Howard Pyle and other members of the Brandywine School came here for inspiration. There's something soothing and soft about the light, maybe because we're surrounded on three sides by ocean and salt is in the air.

You can tell that this is where 'something happened,' a place that has some weight to it. You can feel the gravity. ∎

A LANDSCAPE OF OPPORTUNITY

In the beginning were the Lenni Lanapes, offshoots of the Algonquin, an agricultural people who planted maize in March and, a month afterwards, kidney beans that climbed up the corn like trellises. An early explorer described a Lenape hunt as 'a hundred men lined across a vast field beating bones in their hands to drive animals to the river, where they could be easily killed.' The quality of their clothing was often praised, fashioned out of beaver pelts, feathers from wild turkeys, and deer hair dyed a deep scarlet.

The Dutch were the first Europeans to stake out a presence in Lewes. They acquired from those natives a tract of land extending from Cape Henlopen to the mouth of the Delaware River and, in 1631, started a settlement called Swanendael, 'valley of the swans'. The lure of whales drew them, visions of harvesting a bonanza of precious oil to light the lamps back home. Their venture would prove misguided because whales, it turned out, are scarce off the Delaware coast. Perhaps before they had fully realized their folly, however, tragedy ensued. The thirty-two members of the community, following a series of escalating misunderstandings with the locals, were massacred. Only scarred ashes from their fort was left behind.

Within several decades, however, the Dutch had returned to stay and established a permanent settlement along the banks of the creek now called Hoerekill or 'Harlot's River'. The name, so legend suggests, came from the 'loose' exchanges that transpired along its shore between Dutch men and the native women.

England posted competing claims to the land and relations with the Dutch became increasingly strained. By 1673, Lord Baltimore declared the residents of Whorekill (the English spelling) to be subjects of an enemy nation. That Christmas Eve, 40 soldier horsemen were dispatched with orders to burn every structure and not "leave one stick standing." They accomplished their mission.

Even amongst the English, there was ambiguity about whose charter prevailed here. Maryland and Pennsylvania contested the 'Three Lower Counties on the Delaware.' It would be William Penn, eager to stake out an ocean port for his otherwise land-locked colony, who permanently named the town 'Lewes' (in honor of the location of his family estate in Sussex, England). The drawing of the Mason-Dixon line around 1780 resulted in an independent Delaware that would be the first signer of the United States Constitution.

The strategic position of Lewes, at the cape where the Delaware Bay meets the Atlantic, accounts for much of its history. From early days, the city was an important maritime juncture in the passage of cargo and passengers to Philadelphia, colonial America's commercial and political capital. The river pilots who guided ships trough the treacherous currents of the Bay comprised the town's elite, the builders of many of the imposing houses that still stand along Second Street and Pilottown Road.

In 1700, the notorious Scottish pirate Captain William Kidd anchored off Cape Henlopen for several days. Locals went on board his ship and "received from him and his crew some muslins, calicoes, monies, and other prohibited goods which were from East India." For their actions, these citizens were subsequently arrested as accessories in promoting illegal trade. Legend has it that he buried treasure along the Delmarva coast.

In 1739, George Whitefield, an English contemporary of John Wesley and co-founder of the religious discipline that would become Methodism, arrived in 'Lewis Town' after eleven weeks at sea. Only 24, his flamboyant preaching was already famous and he was invited to deliver a sermon from the pulpit of Anglican St. Peter's. The power of that sermon, and of other influential sermons he delivered in Lewes several months later are, credited with the formation of what is regarded as America's first Methodist Society.

During the Revolutionary War, with Tory

Susie Elkhair of the Delaware Tribe of Indians

sympathizers perhaps as numerous as Patriots in Sussex County, the small fort at Lewes kept British warships out of the Bay. Again, in the War of 1812, Lewes stood as a buffer to British invasion, withstanding off-shore bombardment, protecting the DuPont munitions works outside Wilmington and frustrating the English strategy of launching a front along the Delaware.

Lewes was the setting for one of the engineering wonders of the 19th century, the construction of two vast breakwaters that afforded safety for sailing vessels caught in storm. Work on what is now the inner breakwater began under the administration of President John Quincy Adams, a prime example of the Whig Party's support for large-scale internal improvements that included canals, turnpikes, and harbors. Forty years would be needed to

complete the 1350 foot wall, the first structure of its kind to be built in the western hemisphere. Boulders weighing as much as six tons were brought down from the Palisades of the Hudson River in New York to form a base 160 feet wide that rose fourteen feet above the water line. A second outer breakwater, running for over a mile, was later built to provide even more protection. A description of some two hundred ships sheltering behind the breakwater from a late 19th century gale aptly captures the scale, "a forest of masts moving to and fro as trees bent into the wind."

Another stage in the evolution of Lewes was the construction of Fort Miles on the eve of World War II. Although the Fort never saw military action, the legacy it bequeathed Lewes with its thousands of acres of protected real estate would prove transformational. In 1964, the Department of Defense declared a large portion of the Fort to be surplus. An attempt to privatize the land was thwarted (led in part by a local high school teacher who mobilized a campaign to protect the Great Dune from developers). The state of Delaware stepped in to make it a state park and, today, this 6-mile stretch of unbroken, unsullied beach ranks among the most beautiful on the east coast.

Well into the middle of the twentieth cen-

tury, Lewes was a thriving commercial fishing port. For a number of years more fish tonnage was processed here than anywhere else in the country. Menhaden were harvested by the hundreds of thousands and pressed into oil for soap, paint, and lipstick or pulverized into powder (the name is derived from the native word for 'fertilizer'). "When the wind used to blow out of the southeast," recalled a resident from that era, "the smell was, my God, incredible. It smelled like somebody hadn't washed their feet in ten years." Even though a prolific breeder (a mature female Menhaden produces upwards of 362,000 eggs each season), the waters would be eventually fished out and by the 1960s and the industry here was dead.

What was first regarded as an economic catastrophe, though, would later be seen as a blessing in disguise. Gone was the oppressive smell that had hovered above the town for decades whenever the wind blew wrong and, with its disappearance, life in Lewes took on a new luster.

The shuttered factories were demolished, to be replaced along that prime bay front by the Cape May-Lewes Ferry Terminal and, beginning in the 1980s, the handsome residential communities of Port Lewes and Cape Shores. To some, perhaps, this was a loss of old-time character but hundreds of new

The fabled Menhaden

houses here and in-town at Shipcarpenter Square constituted a powerful shot of economic vitality.

The re-birth of Lewes has continued unabated. Signs of the renaissance abound in stylish shops and restaurants, restored and renovated houses, award-winning public parks and gardens, and even the 20-year-old Nassau Valley Vineyard on the outskirts of town that wins medals in international competitions.

Pilots continue to play an important economic role in the life of the community. They are responsible for guiding shipping from the mouth of the Delaware Bay to ports along the river in Delaware, New Jersey and Pennsylvania---a stretch of 130 miles---and work all matter of vessels from tugboats pulling mammoth barges and fruit ships to naval battleships.

When ships arrive from the ocean, the pilots are taken out to meet them on a craft similar to a large speedboat. The small boat pulls alongside the ship, and the pilot climbs a dangling rope ladder to board the moving vessel. Once on the lower deck, the pilot is escorted directly to the bridge and takes control.

On the return trip out, occasionally a pilot is unable to get off a ship that is exiting the bay in rough seas. When the smaller craft that deliver and pick up pilots are unable to reach a departing ship, the pilot may end up weeks later in a foreign country.

Nowadays, ships loaded with automobiles are regularly brought up the Bay. Millions of barrels of crude oil also are delivered to refineries that stretch from Delaware City to Pennsylvania. Years ago, freighters with coal and grain would come down-river from Philadelphia but now those commodities rarely travel the river.

Amidst four centuries of change, the fundamental spirit of place prevails. Throughout its cycles, Lewes remains a landscape of opportunity tempered by a communal ethic of collective responsibility. It is this very special mix that gets passed down through generations of historical DNA. ∎

Harvesting Menhaden

A Lewes Victorian Girlhood
The Journal of Marjorie Virden, Circa. 1900

Marjorie Virden, the daughter of one of Lewes' first families of river pilots, grew up at the turn of the twentieth century. Throughout much of her youth, she kept a daily diary that is now in the collection of the Lewes Historical Society.

Years later, Judith Akins Roberts described Marjorie in the Journal of the Lewes Historical Society: "There was a maiden lady who lived up the street from us at 334 Pilottown Road with her mother," Ms. Roberts wrote. "I was certain she was a witch. Her hair was always worn in a Dutch bob and was dyed a bright red that seemed to get brighter as she got older ... I once asked her why she wasn't married. She told me she had been married four times but had thrown all her husbands in the 'crik' because she didn't like them."

The entries in her journal recorded common events. Taken as a whole, however, they present a charming portrait of the quotidian reality of a Victorian girlhood in Lewes.

Saturday, Feb 23, 1907:

"I went to quilt and in evening went to club at Mac's. Had hot chocolate, pea-nut butter sandwiches, coffee ice-cream, chocolate lawyer cake, huge cookies, salted peanuts."

Friday, April 4, 1907:

"There is no school as Sara Ewing in our room has scarlet fever."

Friday, November 8, 1907:

"Poor Darling Yellow, Jack Phillip's little 'yeller', died of worms last night."

Wednesday, December 25, 1907:

"Christmas Day! Rained many presents. Good turkey dinner."

Sunday, April 16, 1911:

"I got a lot of nice things for Easter. Mrs. Chambers sent me 2 cakes and a carnation."

Tuesday, October 31, 1911:
"Hurrah. To-night is Halloween. The girls masked up and went to the people of our neighborhood houses. I did not dress up but went to chaperone them."

Wednesday, November 22, 1911:
"I went to Basket Ball practice with Auntie. I like the game very much, though it is tough."

Sunday, December 10, 1911:
"Mamma went away to Phila. To bring Xmas things for me and everybody. I did not go to Sunday School but went to the station."

Wednesday, May 1, 1911:
"We girls made May baskets after school and took them around. Hurrah for May!"

Thursday, May 23, 1911:
"I went to the play called 'The Three Chauffeurs'(in Philadelphia). It was grand. (Especially) the moon-light scene in the tea garden with ladies in handsome dresses and men in full dress suits and high hats. Oh, and music softly crooning and singing. Glorious!"

Wednesday, April 1, 1914:
"April Fool." I fooled every one in our family and Uncle Will. One girl fooled me."

July 20, 1914, Monday:
My Birthday. 15th. My I am getting old. Got several presents. Went to baseball game with Wilmington. Score, 4 to 6 in favor of Lewes."

Wednesday, September 23, 1914:
"Awfully hot. A case of scarlet fever in 5th grade. Room closed. Two more cases of scarlet fever in the afternoon. So no more school this week."

Friday, January 1, 1915:
"New Years Day. Good morning diary. May you bring me lots of love and all good things but no sadness."

Friday, May 14, 1915:
"Dad came home from New York City on evening train. Brought candy, gloves, and baseball magazine and cinnamon bun."

Monday, November 8, 1915:
"Met Ma downtown and we did shopping until late afternoon. In evening Ada G., M, V. and I went to movies and saw Hazel Dawn in "The Fatal Card.""

Saturday, May 11, 1918:
"Roy Wilson came around in the evening. We went to the movies and had a pretty good time. He stayed quite late. I showed him my pictures and he asked for one but I told him he'd have to give me one of his first. I made my mother mad but I can't help it."

HOUSE & GARDEN

L ewes architecture spans the centuries. Some houses here are hundreds of years old, some built yesterday. The remarkable thing, though, is that it's often difficult to tell the difference. This seamless combination of the historic with the modern is the key to 'Lewes style'. Indeed, many consider Lewes one of America's crown jewels in blending the old with the new. The National Historic Trust for Historic Preservation believed so, naming Lewes one of its Dozen Distinctive Destinations in the United States.

The Historic Preservation Commission is charged with maintaining the architectural setting in the Historic District that gives Lewes its celebrated ambiance. Their mandate is as much about encouraging mood as about enforcing regulations. In its own words, the HPC sees its goal "to encourage historical preservation, without discouraging creativity or growth, in keeping with the City's Core Values."

Restoration and Renovation are the twin foundations of Lewes housing. The difference between the two approaches---restoring the old to pristine condition vs. up-dating in form and function--- is more than semantic. By fusing the past with the present, historical authenticity and contemporary creativity are equally served. In their best work, Lewes architects and craftsmen straddle this middle-ground with flair and finesse. ∎

THE ARCHITECTURAL TRADITION IS TO FIT IN WITH THE SURROUNDINGS

Local resident Bill Hiller has long been interested in architecture and for a number of years led architectural walking tours with the Lewes Historical Society.

Lewes is a year round-town and benefits from a different attitude of the homeowners compared to a more typical resort town. The architectural tradition here is to fit in with the surroundings. The owners of fine old houses tend to restore them in keeping with their surroundings rather than tearing them down and building something new.

Lewes architecture is largely what's called 'vernacular,' the kind of design that develops locally. People would hire a carpenter and say 'I want a gable-ended house with a center hall and entry, two rooms downstairs and two rooms upstairs.' That's how most houses got built, by carpenters who knew the standards in the region and used local materials. They might be more plain than those designed by an architect but not necessarily more unsightly.

It is hard from the outside to gauge the age of old houses in Lewes, where unpainted clapboards and shingles soon take on the appearance of age from wind and rain. Plank houses, like the one at the Historical Society grounds, were the earliest houses. They were simple log cabins with the logs squared up into planks.

Later, post-and-beam construction was used. You'd build a foundation by placing rocks or stumps in the ground, then frame the building with four posts and four beams on the perimeter and install diagonal braces so it wouldn't fall down in a windstorm. The joints were mortises and tenons. Making them required big chisels and mallets and good carpentry skills.

The 19th century building where Azafran Café is located was renovated some years ago and when the exterior siding came off, you could see posts and beams with Roman numerals chiseled into them, showing which beam went on which post. The fabrication of the building was probably done elsewhere and then carted to Market Street by wagon for assembly.

Things changed when the industrial revolution came into full flower. Before, you'd go out into the forest, cut down a tree, and hew the wood yourself. Then came the steam engine and you could run boards through a mill that could be where the trees were and not tied to a source of waterpower. This led to dimension lumber, 2x4s and 4x4s and the like. Framing methods changed. With post and beam, you could build a rectangle pretty easily but anything more elaborate was difficult. Now, with dimension lumber and wire nails, you could build a house in any shape you liked.

The railroad came to Lewes at the very end of 1869, the first passengers were picked up on New Years Day 1870 in a station located where the Library is today. The arrival of the railroad prompted a building boom. Victorian style ornamentation---columns, balustrades, brackets, and decorative panels—could be produced by machinery, ordered from a catalogue, and shipped to Lewes by train. The embellishments on the porches that were added on to houses along Mulberry Street were probably constructed this way.

The Scott Building (205 Second Street), which houses the Biblion bookstore is probably my favorite building in town. It was built in 1885 in the Italianate style by Robert Scott, a tinsmith who set up business in Lewes after the Civil War making things like kitchen implements, cookie cutters, and stove pipes. His big success came from selling stoves, which were commonly used in that era to heat individual rooms. The building was 'high style' at the time, with a raised townhouse to the left of the shop. The architect was the famous Frank Furness of Philadelphia, who designed the Grand Opera House and the old Pennsylvania Railroad Station (now Amtrak) in Wilmington. There's still great marble ornamentation around the windows, brackets under the eaves, and glazed bricks that enliven a plain wall by providing a band of dark, shiny green.

The Buttery at Second Street and Savannah Road was built in the Queen Anne style in 1890 by a river pilot named Morris and represents the culmination of the Victorian architecture. The woodwork inside is original.

The purple house next door, now Ocean Retreat Day Spa (210 Savannah Road), was built by a salvage diver. Ships that sought shelter in winter storms behind the breakwater would often lose their anchor and Captain Johnson would retrieve them in the spring to sell as scrap iron. The house has what's called a 'belly porch' on the front. Successful people of that era would dine out-doors so they could be seen and set an example for others to aspire to. There's also an inset porch above the main entry. Such porches were common because many families had a member who suffered from tuberculosis. It was called a 'consumptive porch.' The sick person could sit there to take the air.

Much of the new construction in Lewes today is beyond Fourth Street in what was historically the African-American area of town. There's still some small houses there but most of them are gone. The occupants tended to be renters and lost their leases when the property owners, during the housing boom prior to 2008, found they could sell their properties for upwards of half a million dollars. ∎

'THE LEWES STYLE'

Architectural Designer Brenda B. Jones grew up in Lewes and has been involved in the construction and renovation of a large number of houses here. She is noted for a clean, understated approach that harmonizes different elements into a graceful whole.

We asked her to select a sampler of houses that exemplify 'the Lewes Style.'

By Brenda Jones

624 PILOTTOWN ROAD

This proud historical house reflects classic elements of 1800's architectures with the balanced symmetry, windows evenly spaced on both levels, and cypress siding.

630 PILOTOWN ROAD

This is great architecture for Lewes, it shows how a large house can maintain size and scale, take advantage of canal views, and not overwhelm the surroundings.

20 SHIPCARPENTER SQUARE

The combination restoration/renovation moved the historic lighthouse from its original site to this location, as many Lewes houses have been picked up and moved.

415 BURTON AVENUE

Narrow Lewes lots (40x100) favored 'shot gun' houses. This updated classic embodies farm-cottage elements (high windows, board & batten siding, dormers).

124 KINGS HIGHWAY

This house was assembled from a turn-of-the-twentieth century Sears mail order building kit.

536 PILOTTOWN

Dutch colonial Maull House (circa. 1750) with signature gambrel sloped roof.

330 MARKET STREET

Gothic Revival Cottage style with two gables is very rare, this is the only one in Lewes.

340 MARKET STREET

Classic Second Empire with intricate, brightly painted woodwork trim.

321 THIRD STREET

This very little cottage was renovated and expanded in keeping with Historic Register dictates that when you restore, you should be able to 'lift apart' the new portions and leave the old section (on the left) intact.

111 W. CANAL

Typical 'old' Lewes beach house, 1½ story bungalow.

POKE A STICK INTO THE GROUND AND IT WILL GROW

So goes the local claim. A bit of an exaggeration, perhaps, but the climate, soil, and conditions here make Lewes ideal for lush landscapes. Situated at a 'zone of transition,' the area's location is conducive to both northern and southern plants.

This is a town where gardening is a matter of civic pride. All the more so since 2003, when Lewes in Bloom, a volunteer organization that tends many public plantings, won first prize in a national contest for city beautification. The first Tulip Festival was held a few years later and

Fisher-Martin Herb Garden

has since morphed into an annual spring extravaganza displaying more than 10,000 bulbs in parks and public spaces. In 2012, the continuing horticultural excellence` of Lewes' gardeners was further recognized when it received the great honor of being named to America In Bloom's national Circle of Champions.

Private gardens are equally ambitious. The traditional English influence, with its emphasis on boxwoods, provided the foundation for bolder initiatives drawing on plants native to the region like sweet gum trees, river birch, willow oaks, bald cypress and bayberry shrubs. The 19th century interest in Asian plants (crape myrtle, Japanese magnolia) took place early here because of familiarity with international influences by way of the port. The arrival the past few years of residents whose tastes were shaped elsewhere has rendered traditional gardens more sophisticated with new varieties and species, often displayed in dense drifts of planting. ■

SOUTHERN MAGNOLIA

Because magnolias appeared on the scene before bees, the tree is pollinated by beetles that are drawn to the showy flower's high protein pollen as food. Migrating songbirds also find magnolia seeds a prime source of energy.

The genus was first spotted by a French explorer in Martinique in 1703 and named after naturalist Pierre Magnol, one of the inventors of botanical classifications. By the end of the 18th century, specimens of these broad-leaved evergreens, often collected from China and Japan, had become popular in fashionable gardens.

CRAPE MYRTLE

Conditions in Lewes are ideal for Crape Myrtle trees, which abound here in various colors and sizes. These fast growing trees annually shed the previous year's outer bark in summer to reveal beautiful, new bark giving the trunk its distinctive mottled appearance.

Native to the Indian subcontinent and southeast Asia, they were first brought to America in 1790 by Andre Michaux and were known to be cultivated at Mount Vernon. Michaux travelled around the world for the King of France, scouting for trees with which to quickly rebuild the country's forests that had had been decimated by wars with England. He was also responsible for introducing the Camilla, mimosa, and gardenia to America.

PRICKLY PEAR CACTUS

Prickly pear cactus grows wild on the secondary or back dunes along the beach, especially off to the left of Cape Henlopen Drive in an area referred to as "Prickly Pear Park." The plant has developed a waxy coating that protects it from insects, salt, sand winds, and water evaporation.

Yellow flowers appear in the summer, which turn into edible purple fruit by fall. Native Americans, who roasted or dried them and then grounded them into flour, prized these 'pears'. They also used the plump pads to dress wounds.

BLACK-EYED SUSAN

Swaths of Black-Eyed Susan combined with naturalized plantings provide drama to many a Lewes garden (and many a roadside field). They grow quickly, are very competitive and push other plants out of an area. These biennial daisies are members of the sunflower family, sending up flower stalks their second year and then dying.

The Black-Eyed Susan figured in the 'secret' vocabulary of flowers to the Victorians. Depending on the context, it conveyed encouragement, impartiality, and even 'pure' love.

YARROW

In the last several decades, contemporary garden designs in Lewes have seized upon ornamental drifts of Yarrow as companions to provide accent. Flower heads, some twenty to twenty-five in compact clusters, appear at the top of three-foot stems.

The plant has long been used for its healing powers, particularly to encourage clotting for cuts and abrasions. The genus name, Achillea, is derived from the Greek hero Achilles who reputedly carried it with his army to treat wounds. Several birds---the starling, the tree swallow---line their nests with yarrow, experiments suggest this inhibits the growth of parasites.

RIVER BIRCH

A local native, the River Birch thrives in a wet, moist habitat. While too contorted and knotty to be of much value as lumber, it bark makes it an ornamental favorite for landscapers. Native Americans boiled its sap as a sweetener and ate the inner bark as survival food. The life span of the River Birch is shorter than many other trees---but it grows faster.

KNOCK OUT ROSES

Knock Out roses, a new breed of hardy rose bush bred to require little maintenance, are increasingly playing a starring role in local gardens. Easy to grow, they survive Lewes' hot, humid climate much better than more traditional Hybrid Tea Roses and are bred for disease resistance.

The bushes bloom vibrant red, yellow or pink flowers every five to six weeks and are 'self-cleaning,' automatically releasing dead flowers so there is no need for deadheading.

HYDRANGEA

A renaissance of the Hydrangea is occurring in Lewes, with loyalty running deep to old fashioned varieties like 'Niko Blue' with its stunning nine-inch flowers. The flower color depends on soil acidity, the more the acid the deeper the blue (while blooms in more alkaline soil are lighter, even pink).

A GARDEN TOUR THROUGH THE HISTORIC DISTRICT

Brenda Brady, Sussex County Master Gardener and co-founder of Lewes in Bloom.

Lewes is celebrated as a town where gardens have become a passion. The conditions are ideal. Equally important in making Lewes a city of natural beauty has been the work and example of Lewes in Bloom, a volunteer organization devoted to cultivating the town's public gardens as well as planters at the foot of the Savannah Road bridge over the canal.

We asked Brenda Brady, Sussex County Master Gardener and co-founder of Lewes in Bloom, to guide a walk through the Historic District pointing out notable aspects of gardens visible along the way.

A 3 Shipcarpenter Square - Roses, azaleas and perennials. **B** 27 Shipcarpenter Square - Roses and trees. **C** 20 Shipcarpenter Square - Boxwoods, roses and perennials. **D** 34 Shipcarpenter Square - Shrubs and small trees. **E** 409 St. Paul Street - A Fringe Tree

F 320 Mulberry Street - A Japanese Maple and box-woods. **G** 326 Mulberry Street - A front garden with a picket fence and a variety of flowers. **H** 425 Park Avenue - A nice assortment of shrubs, annuals, and perennials. **I** 10 Shipcarpenter Square - A magnolia, roses and shrubs. **J** 423 Park Avenue - A diversion of trees, shrubs and perennials. **K** 407 St. Paul Street - Roses and shrubs. **L** 307 West Third Street - A courtyard garden planted with shrubs, perennials

LIVING LEWES
Tours

'X MARKS THE SPOT' THE HEART OF LEWES

TOURS BEGIN IN ST. PETER'S SQUARE, AT THE INTERSECTION OF SECOND STREET AND MARKET STREET

Walking Tour South (PAGE 48) routes through Gazebo Square to the Cannonball House, then a block up Savannah Road to the Zwaanendael Museum.

Walking Tour North (PAGE 60) wanders through the St. Peters churchyard to the Historical Society Complex, then the architectural wizardry of Ship Carpenter's Square, past African-American landmarks to a 1700s former Methodist meeting house now rumored to be haunted.

Wheels (Bike/Car) to Sunset Point (PAGE 74) rolls over the canal through the boatyards and bait shops of 'Fisherman's Pier' to the town beach on the Bay and past water-front cottages to west-ward facing Roosevelt Inlet.

Wheels to the Windmill (PAGE 84) rolls out Pilottown Road along the Canal to the monument where the first settlers put down, into the University of Delaware's College of Ocean, Earth and the Environment and through woods to the base of the wind turbine.

Wheels to Rehoboth (PAGE 82) for bikes only (sorry!) out a pastoral country road to the rail-trail through piney wetlands and expansive farmlands six miles to Rehoboth.

Anchoring the square is King's Ice Cream, a legendary landmark.

Lore has it that the shop spurred the town's 're-birth' when Tom King and wife Chris opened a Lewes branch of the family's Milton, Delaware ice cream parlor in 1981, providing a reason for people to come downtown after dark.

Viewed from a bench in front of King's, one looks across at the red-brick Rodney Hotel.

Now a fashionable boutique hotel with a designer-chic lobby that defines Lewes' version of metro trendiness, the Rodney has been around since 1926 and used to be known as the Zwaanendael Inn. Looking to the right, is Biblion Used Books and Rare Finds, a most welcoming new-ish addition (2011) with an ever-changing collection of selectively curated 'pre-owned' books at affordable prices and a comfy couch that invites you to start reading. ∎

Walking Tour, South

Heading south from St. Peter's Square, Lewes unfolds in its full sweep. The richness of the town's overlapping textures peel away. Shops, restaurants and museums await the visitor.

History abounds along this walk. Cannon emplacements face seaward, reminders of the fort that stood here to keep the British from sailing up the Bay. Artifacts from the era of clipper ships are in the maritime museum in the Cannonball House. The stepped-gables and tiled roof of Zwaanendael Museum are modeled after a 17th century Dutch town hall.

There's an array of delicacies to sample along the way from the one-of-a-kind 'ooey-gooey' invented at the Lewes Bake Shoppe (along with a cup of coffee from beans freshly roasted on the premises) to exotic smoothies at Nectar Café and Juice Bar. Kid's Ketch might be as good a toy store as exists anywhere. The clothes and home furnishing shops on Front Street and Second display a level of style not to be expected in a little Delaware coastal town. ∎

Pilottown Rd

W Market St

Front St.

Bank St.

Nells Alley

Second St.

Market St.

Chestnut St.

Third St.

Savannah Rd

Kings Hwy

1

2

3

4

5

6

7

8

N

MARY VESSELS PARK
"GAZEBO SQUARE" (Map #1)

At the end of Market Street, which takes its name from the historic marketplace that long stood here adjacent to the creek (now the canal), stands 'Gazebo Square.' The park is named in honor of Mary Vessels, the first Chair of the Lewes Parks and Recreation Committee and the person credited with taking the lead in rehabilitating Second Street.

Fort Horn Kill, the encampment established under orders of New Netherlands Governor Peter Stuyvesant in 1659, was located nearby and is marked by a plaque. Although the Dutch would be dispossessed, they were followed a few years later by a colony of Amsterdam Mennonites whose descendants remain a presence in Sussex County.

The Inn at Canal Square provides a tone of Nantucket to the setting. Come the shank of the day, folks sip from the wine bar selection and eat gourmet mini-pizzas at Half Full.

The Square hosts various events, including the October Fest, but its chief claim to fame is the welcoming shelter of the gazebo beneath a giant magnolia tree, the perfect spot for slackers to read the newspaper or sip a lemonade. It's also an ideal location to unloose children from the tyranny of smart phones and allow them to exercise their fantasy.

SECOND STREET (Map #3)

Dodd's Corner, the building that houses Agave Restaurant, was the town's general store and principal ship chandler throughout the 19th century.

Across the street you'll see the old 19th century Sussex Trust bank building, an interesting edifice with a false classical front that, when seen from the side in profile, could be a Hollywood set.

Kid's Ketch is most magical, started by a Lewes mother frustrated with the toy choices available at the Big Box Stores. Among the 'all-time' popular items for shoppers of all ages are the flying monkey, the stomp rocket, fashion headbands and Suspend Game.

A few doors up is Lewes' Bakery Shoppe and Notting Hill Coffee Roasters. Besides croissants, quiche, and Gorilla Sticks, this is the home of the Ooey Gooey! The old-time roaster on the side isn't a prop, the coffee you drink here has been roasted in-house.

CANNONBALL HOUSE (Map #2)

Known as the Rowland House, this building is a rare example of a Lewes house that has remained on one site for it's entire existence (moving houses is relatively easy here because the land is so flat). It was built circa 1769. During the War of 1812, this was the home of Gilbert McCracken and his son Henry who served in a volunteer militia composed primarily of Delaware Bay pilots that defended Lewes. During the bombardment of the town on April 6 and April 7, 1813, the house was struck by a cannonball---which remains lodged in its brick (truth in advertising, it's a small cannonball).

In past lives the structure has been a restaurant, laundry and even the mayor's office. It was saved from destruction in 1961 when a group of local citizens gathered together one evening to share concern that the town was losing its heritage. Thus was born the Lewes Historical Society.

Inside you'll find artifacts celebrating Lewes' four century kinship with the sea, including a Spanish pirate's chest and exhibition rooms with storyboards, pictures and objects themed to different phases of Lewes' history. The 'gem' of the collection is the giant 14-foot lens from an old lighthouse.

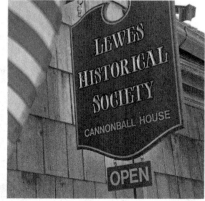

War of 1812

In the second year of the war, frustrated militarily in its Great Lakes campaign, the British launched a second front attacking the mid-Atlantic coast. A major tactical objective was to disrupt and commandeer the Delaware 'bread basket' responsible for much American food supply.

Two frigates and several smaller vessels were dispatched to blockade the entrance to the Delaware Bay and support the landing of troops in the interior. Soon after taking their position within sight of Lewes, the British issued an order to the townsfolk to provide them with provisions. The Commodore of the squadron, J. Beresford, sent the following demand to 'the first magistrate' of the town:

"As soon as you receive this, I must request you will send twenty live bullocks (or bulls), with a proportionate quantity of vegetables and hay for the use of his Britannic Majesty's squadron, now at this anchorage, to be immediately paid for at the Philadelphia prices. If you refuse to comply with this request, I shall be under the necessity of destroying your town."

The demand was rejected. On April 8, the British attempt to land soldiers on the shore was repulsed. With that, Beresford ordered a bombardment. Two hundred and forty-one guns fired upon the town in twenty-two hours. Although property was damaged, no injuries were incurred. An historian writing some 75 years later speculated that the town escaped extensive damage because "the trees on the marsh of Lewes Beach obstructed the view (of the attackers) to such an extent that their aim was not effective."

The tenacious locals scored a victory in preventing the British fleet from continuing up the Delaware River, thereby saving the likely attack on the DuPont Powder Mills and perhaps even Philadelphia. ■

FRONT STREET (Map #4)
1812 Memorial Park and City Dock

The fort at Lewes during the Revolutionary War and War of 1812 stood here, the spot marked by a granite monument placed by the National Society, US Daughters of 1812.

Four large guns were contributed by the US government with a smaller gun believed to be taken from an abandoned pirate vessel.

This park is a great vantage point to catch the waning sun in the late afternoon.

SAVANNAH ROAD & SECOND STREET (Map #5)

TOUCH OF ITALY
(101 Second Street)

A combination top-of-the-line Italian gourmet deli, bakery, and restaurant (with a cozy bar in the corner). A hall of gastronomic delights smacking of ethnic authenticity to a soundtrack of Frank Sinatra and Dean Martin.

LEWES MERCANTILE ANTIQUES
(109 Second Street)

Over 30 dealers provide a revolving inventory of collectibles from antique to kitsch. Great shopping for architectural pieces, estate jewelry, old maps and furniture, silverware, glassware, textiles, umbrellas from Thailand, oriental carpets. You name it!

SHOREBREAK
(115 Savannah Road)

Casual coastal men's wear with an eye to classic style updated in a contemporary idiom at a surprisingly modest price points. Range of 'laid back' ware from sweaters and shirts to eccentric objects like game fish bottle openers.

ZWAANENDAEL MUSEUM (Map #7)

This showcase for local maritime, military, and social history was built in 1932 to celebrate Lewes' 300th anniversary and was named for the first European settlement in the state of Delaware, a Dutch whaling colony called Swaanendael (Valley of the Swans) begun in 1631 along the shore of Lewes Creek.

The building is a replica of the town hall of Hoorn, Holland, home of David DeVries, the merchant captain who was a sponsor of that original colony and the leader in its founding. His statue stands on the roof. The architecture features such typically 17th century Dutch elements as stepped gables, terra cotta roof tiles, and decorated shutters.

Entrance is free (donations always welcome!). Inside are exhibits about the Swanendael settlement, Cape Henlopen Lighthouse, the bombardment of Lewes by the British in the War of 1812, pilots of the Delaware River and Bay, and the ever-changing Delaware coastline. There are also finds from sunken ships, pottery, and examples of maritime archaeology.

Operating hours at the Zwaanendael Museum are 10 a.m. to 4:30 p.m., Wednesdays through Saturdays, from Nov. 1 to March 31; and 10 a.m. to 4:30 p.m., Tuesdays through Saturdays, and 1:30 to 4:30 p.m. on Sundays from April 1 to Oct. 31.

A special exhibition runs in 2013, "A Seaborne Citizenry: The DeBraak and Its Atlantic World" about Delaware's most famous shipwreck. The HMS DeBraak was a two-masted brig sloop, a class of ship used extensively in the Napoleonic period against privateers. In 1798, it sank in a sudden squall in Delaware Bay loaded with Spanish bounty. Salvage efforts finally located the sunken ship in 1984 and produced 20,000 artifacts which the state purchased, a sampling of which are on display.

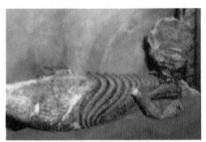

Spanish coins from the DeBraak

Upstairs, check out the Merman, an example of sailor's folk-art made in China in the mid-19th century of fish, hair, ivory, and a shrunken monkey head. Captains returning from newly opened Oriental ports, would prank the gullible with tall tales of 'never-be-fore-seen' creatures such as this.

GRAND VICTORIANS (Map #6)

Several imposing Victorian houses at the corner of Savannah and Second serve as the town welcoming committee, elegant reminders of the town's prosperity in the late-1800s.

Ocean Day Spa (210 Savannah) building dates from 1896 and is renowned for a crafted period staircase wending up to the second floor. The extension of the verandah was known as a 'belly porch', a space where grand Victorians dined 'en plein air' to see and be seen.

ZWAANENDAEL WOMEN'S CLUB

The Zwannendael Women's Club was organized over a century ago to promote community involvement. Among its first accomplishments was contributing to the successful effort to pass child labor laws in Delaware in 1913. It continues to support volunteer activities, make charitable donations, and provide scholarships. Its present home, the former Sussex Trust Title and Safe Deposit Company office, was built in 1898 and is listed on the National Register of Places.

FISHER-MARTIN HOUSE (Map #8)

This charming historic house, dating from the 1730's, was moved here from Cool Spring, Delaware (Route 9 toward Georgetown) as part of the 350th anniversary of the first European settlement in 1980.

It now houses the Lewes Chamber of Commerce and Visitors Bureau. Various artifacts are on display but the real attraction is the physical house itself, a prime example of how rural gentry lived in the 18th and 19th centuries.

The award-winning garden nearby has been cultivated to resemble a Colonial housewife's medicinal and culinary herb garden.

FISHER-MARTIN HERB GARDEN

The garden at the Fisher-Martin House, (seen on pages 38 and 39) was entirely re-planted in 2007 by Lewes in Bloom volunteers with medicinal and culinary plants and herbs commonly found in 1700's colonial Delmarva.

The inner four areas contain some fifty different herbs used by housewives for medicine, to strew on the floor to 'de-odorize' the house with pleasing fragrances, to protect clothing by repelling moths, for flavoring salad, and coloring fabric.

Among the plantings are Lady's Bedstraw, whose tops were used for stuffing bed sacks as the scent killed fleas. Soapwort, used for making soap, has a beautiful pink flower. Clary sage was a relaxant for stress, asthma, and to help digestion. Pheasant's Eye, which slows the heartbeat causing it to pump blood more efficiently, could be used to treat arrhythmic 'nervous heart' and mild heart failure as well as cramps and menstrual disorders. Narcissi were taken for whopping cough. Salad Burnet's leaves contain vitamin C, aid digestion and give a nutty flavor to salads, soft cheese, soups and salad dressing.

In the dyeing garden is True Indigo, a shrub whose leaves are processed to produce the distinctive color mid-way between blue and purple. The American variety of Elderberry, whose berries could provide sustenance for weeks and were much prized by Native Americans, produces a golden yellow coloring. Madder is another dye plant that yields red, pink and brown dyes. The yellow flower heads of Tansy are used for golden dye and the leaves are a powerful bug repellent for ants, fleas and flies.

WALKING TOUR, NORTH

This tour leads the visitor into the spirit of Lewes through historic churchyard gravestones, structures that date back centuries, and even a lighthouse converted into a residence.

This is a walk to savor. It is a journey into timelessness.

The courtyard of St. Peter's contains stones from the 1700s, including the grave of a sea captain buried with his anchor. A bookshop for 'spiritual seekers' of all faiths nestles in a tranquil setting along with meditation labyrinth. The oldest house in America still on its original foundation is on the walk, as well as the grand Victorians of Second Street.

The Historical Society grounds include vintage 19th century buildings.

Shipcarpenter Square is a residential development of historic homes moved from other locations, restored, and updated. The original Old Bethel Church was a 'one room preaching house' where America's earliest Methodists gathered. ■

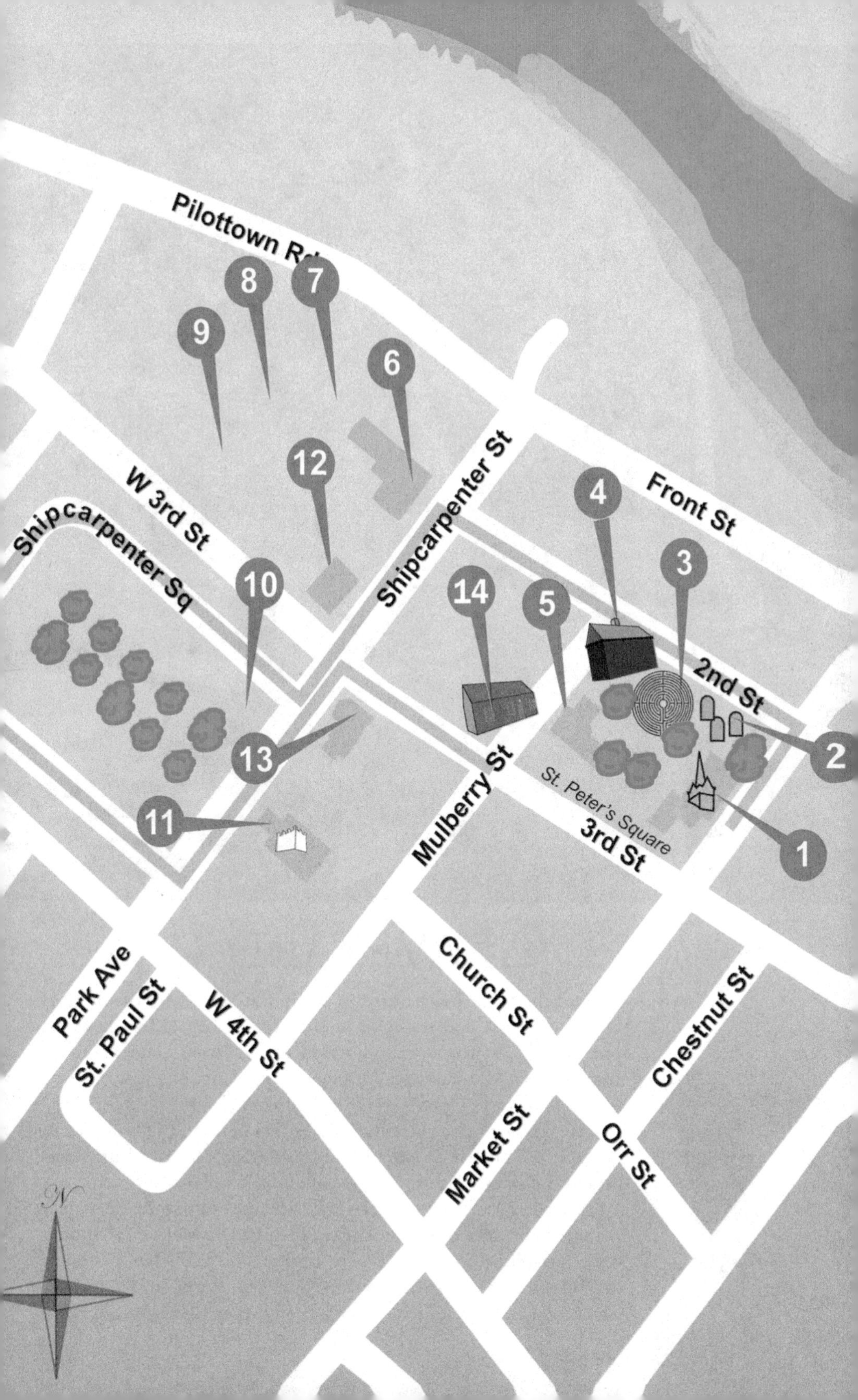

Pilottown Rd

8

7

9

6

12

W 3rd St

Shipcarpenter St

Shipcarpenter Sq

4

Front St

14

5

3

2nd St

10

13

2

11

Mulberry St

St. Peter's Square

3rd St

1

Church St

Park Ave

St. Paul St

W 4th St

Market St

Orr St

Chestnut St

N

GRAVEYARD (Map #2)

Captain James Drew

Beyond the brick wall bordering Second Street, where the original Sussex County Court was built in 1680 for the cost of five thousand pounds of tobacco, is the graveyard of St. Peter's. The walkways amongst the old stones wend through an ambiance of serene, historic repose. The earliest grave is that of Margaret Huling, born in 1631.

Four Governors of Delaware lie buried here, the first physician in the state (a native of Ireland), judges, legislators and many members of the Maull and Rodney families.

Henry E. McCracken (1791-1868) was a pilot from the days when a single man went out alone miles off shore to await an in-coming vessel (established practice gave the commission to the first person to step on the deck of an arriving ship). A violent storm kicked up. McCracken's sole hope was to set anchor and pray that it would hold.

The anchor held. As a gesture of his eternal gratitude, McCracken willed that the anchor be buried with him, a trace of which still pokes through the ground.

Another noteworthy grave is that of Captain James Drew, commander of the British war ship DeBraak which foundered off Cape Henlopen in 1798. A sculpted marble urn sits atop his handsome tomb, inscribed to one "beloved for his virtue and admired for his bravery."

Among the tallest markers is that of Captain Henry Virden (1815-1884). Following the loss of the schooner Enoch Turley, with six pilots and more apprentices aboard, Virden organized the local pilots into a collaborative association that would no longer compete for commissions but rather allocate assignments in an orderly way so pilots need not put themselves at risk. His home, now a highly rated B&B famous for gourmet breakfasts, stands directly across at 217 Second Street.

Captain Henry Virden

ST. PETER'S EPISCOPAL CHURCH (Map #1)

St. Peter's Parish was founded in 1681, by a group of citizens who petitioned the Governor for four acres of land at the center of Lewes to establish a Church of England congregation. Two structures preceded the current Gothic revival church, which was constructed from 1854-1858 and occupies a portion of the original land grant.

The doors of the church are open twenty-four hours a day, providing continuous sanctuary for quiet reflection. The organ is particularly renowned, re-built in a multi-year renovation beginning in 1998 to add digital voices and additional stops to create a most concert-worthy instrument.

LABRYNTH (Map #3)

The 'Path of Peace' labyrinth provides a healing, restorative tool to those who partake of its ancient symbolism. It was erected in the churchyard of St. Peter's to offer a 'walking meditation.' Walking the labyrinth serves as a kind of metaphor for a spiritual journey, a path that leads to the same source regardless of where one enters. Visitors are encouraged to focus on an intention as they begin, then to 'let go of stresses, concerns, and expectations' as they move onward. It is customary to leave a memento at the center as a token of gratitude.

SEEKERS (Map #5)

The mission of this 'one-of-a-kind' gift shop is ecumenical, taking its name from the Gospel of Matthew ("Ask and you will receive. Seek and you will find."). Here one finds an assortment of inter-faith books about worship, family, grief counseling and spiritual development. Particularly interesting are Haitian wall sculptures inspired by the artist's dreams of loss from the earthquake (sales support Haiti's re-building).

The shaded seating in front is a welcome resting place to enjoy the tranquil setting.

RYVES HOLT HOUSE (Map #4)

The original façade of this building is to the right and may be the oldest structure in the United States still standing on its original foundation. It was built 1665 owned by Ryves Holt, the first chief justice of the "Three Lowers Counties on the Delaware" from 1745 until his death in 1763. Leased by the Lewes Historical Society, this is now an information center about forthcoming tours, lectures, festivals and shows. A variety of quaint, quirky articles---antique in feeling if not fact---are for sale. While inside, be sure to check out the uncovered original wall that exposes how 'mortar mud' was poured between the planks to secure and seal them.

SECOND STREET TO HISTORICAL SOCIETY GROUNDS

Second Street walking north from St. Peter's Square is the grand promenade of historic Lewes. Depending on the time and day, the mood can be quiet or animated. Either way, this unique setting is always absorbing with houses that embody the span of American architecture from colonial restoration to contemporary renovation.

215 Second Street displays Victorian elements, with its steeped roof and porch details. The elegant wooden filigree nestled into the high pointed gable at the peak of the roof is a fine example of 'high' Victorian ornamentation.

217 Second Street (Virden House) and the next two (221, 223) are handsome houses that were all built by ship pilots, evidence to the prominence of these figures. Circa 1888.

217 Second Street

221 Second Street evokes the work of Frank Lloyd Wright and suggests that its architect was acquainted with the Prairie School in the overhanging of the flat second floor roof and widow pane designs. The broad, curving wrap-around verandah is one of town's nicest.

221 Second Street

226 Second Street dates from the early 1800s and has been beautifully renovated. Next at 232, the siding is probably the original slat shingles made from cedar trees, which commonly grew in this area and were prized for their resistance to decay from moisture and insects. Circa 1860.

227 Second Street is joined with post-and-beam construction, the practice before the industrial revolution improved metallurgy techniques so steel could be drawn out into long wire and made into nails.

226 Second Street

236 Second Street is 'two houses in one,' composed of a post-and-beam structure (on the right) around which was later built a much larger balloon frame structure.

231 Second Street is a classic grey Federal style house characterized by plain but handsome exterior, symmetric balance and an ornate entryway.

241 Second Street is an example of the 'Lewes Style' that blends new with old with such respect that it is difficult to tell the original part of the house from the addition.

236 Second Street

LEWES HISTORICAL SOCIETY COMPLEX

A group of citizens, concerned at the deteriorating state of Lewes' 19th century houses, were sailing along the Canal one day in 1961 when they observed the terrible condition of Rowland House with its embedded cannonball from the War of 1812. So legend goes, they decided on the spot to do something to preserve Lewes' legacy. A few months later, the Lewes Historical Society was established.

Subsequently, the lot at Third and Shipcarpenter Streets was purchased and designated the Historic Complex. Since then, ten structures have been re-located here.

The Society, led by Executive Director Michael DiPaolo, does more than maintain buildings, however. It actively keeps Lewes' past vibrant with meetings, events, proceedings, scholarship and publications.

HIRAM RODNEY BURTON HOUSE (Map #6)

Built on lands that sold for 3000 pounds of tobacco in 1675, the Hiram Rodney Burton House at the northern end of Second Street has presided over Lewes for more than three centuries. It houses the offices of the Lewes Historical Society.

The Chear House, as it was known on early land deeds, passed through the family of James Wildtbank, a rector of St. Peter's Church in the early 1700s and then served as a tenant house for boarders. The property was sold in 1814 to neighboring landowner Thomas Rodney, a privateer, or legal pirate licensed by the U.S. to plunder British ships in the War of 1812.

The grand house at the end of Second Street is now fittingly named for Dr. Hiram Rodney Burton, a physician of imposing height at six feet six inches, who would leave a lasting legacy when, as a U.S. Congressman (1905-1909), he secured federal funds that helped create the modern-day Lewes-Rehoboth Canal. Before his death, Dr. Burton set aside much of his Southwestern property for the growing African-American community in Lewes, creating the Burton subdivision neighborhood in 1923. The house operated briefly as the Maple Shade Tea Room and was then a private residence until 1989, when the Lewes Historical Society acquired the building and grounds.

Inside is a collection of donated antiques, maps and display materials.

THE SCHOOLHOUSE (Map #7)

The sea-foam green, fish-scale shingled Midway School House #178 educated local farm kids who lived between Lewes and Rehoboth from 1898 to 1937 at its former location near the present Rehoboth Mall. Each year, around 20 students traveled three to five miles from surrounding areas to be educated through eighth grade, or until their family needed full-time help on the farm (class sizes in the upper grades typically dwindled for this reason).

Boys and girls sat separately on the benches. When their grade was called, they went to the front for the day's lesson while the other students practiced lessons on their own. This helped students refresh their memories of old lessons as they moved on to higher grade levels.

The school day ran from 8 a.m. to 4 p.m. Upon arrival, students deposited their coats and lunch pails in the front alcove, next to the water pail and a pile of wood for the stove that remains inside. The windows are original, the same through which turn-of-the-century students surely daydreamed.

On Farmer's Market Saturday mornings the Children's Librarian from Lewes Public Library holds a story session here, typically beginning at 9:30 (please confirm at www.historiclewes-farmersmarket.org)

RABBIT'S FERRY HOUSE (Map #8)

Sided in native Sussex County cypress shake shingles, the Rabbit's Ferry House is named for the small rural community north of Lewes where it was built. The farmhouse was saved from demolition in 1967 and moved here as an example of early colonial architecture. The original one-room, oak timber dwelling with a sleeping loft dates to 1741. The entrance, stairway, living room, upstairs hall and two adjoining rooms were added later in the 18th century. Most of the windowpanes, once known as "lights," have the telltale imperfections of old glass.

Furnished with authentic Sussex County antiques both on loan and donated by supporters, Rabbit's Ferry House is actively used throughout the year for plant sales, antiques bazaars, Christmas tours and even ghost hunts.

DOCTOR'S OFFICE (Map #9)

This old doctor's office was a fixture in downtown Lewes starting in the 1830s, located at various times on Savannah Road, Second, and Market Streets. From its thick Doric columns to its lofty apex, the old office is the only remaining example in Lewes of the Greek Revival architecture that was popular throughout America in the early to mid-1800s.

A collection of artifacts and 19th century medical tools remain in the waiting room and physician's office, including an actual human skull and apothecary jars that contained popular medications of the day such as quinine (treatment for malaria, originally discovered by Peruvian tribes to halt shivering due to low temperatures), snake oil (prescribed widely to cure any disease, smooth wrinkles, remove stains, prolong life or treat any number of common ailments) and peroxide (used in the 1800s not only for sterilization but as treatment for syphilis and tuberculosis).

Much of the antique medical equipment on display has been curated by the Historical Society to tell the story of how medicine advanced during the lifetime of the old doctor's office. The prosthetic legs with hinges for joints represented cutting-edge technology at the time of the Civil War. "The crazy thing," observes Historical Society Executive Director Michael DiPaolo, "is that we've had doctors come in who say that, other than not being made of steel anymore, lots of things haven't changed that much."

SHIPCARPENTER SQUARE (Map #10)

The vintage houses of Shipcarpenter Square were moved from elsewhere and grouped around a spacious commons making it one of America's most unique subdivisions. Its development, beginning in the early 1980s, marks a significant moment in the renaissance of Lewes.

This land between Third and Fourth Streets used to be a ball field and picnic grounds used by the surrounding African-American neighborhood, a neighborhood known as 'Ca-May' because of the abundance of wild chamomile plants that grew here. Legend has it that when there was talk of a developer building build condos here, locals Jack Vessels and David Dunbar countered with a concept of a community restricted to re-located structures (circa 1899 and earlier). The landholder, Otis Smith who owned the manhaden fish processing plants and served eighteen years as Mayor of Lewes, preferred that idea.

By deed and custom, homeowners remain committed to maintaining the spirit of authenticity as they 'modernize' and expand the small historic houses that were moved here intact or dismantled and reassembled from throughout Sussex County.

Of particular interest is a house (20 Shipcarpenter Square) with attached cylindrical lighthouse tower, a replica of the Mispillion Lighthouse constructed with original remnants. Built in 1831 to guide vessels up-river from the Bay to Milton, the lighthouse was deactivated in 1929 and ultimately destroyed by lightning.

1831

Today

ST. GEORGE'S AFRICAN METHODIST EPISCOPAL CHURCH

317 Park Avenue (Map #11)

St. George's AME is the oldest African-American church in the Lewes area, established in 1816. It sits on a lot that once adjoined burial ground deeded to the Episcopal Church. The present church was built in 1883.

301 THIRD/PARK STREET
(Map #13)

This is the only house in Lewes with a diagonal front door. Why? It was done for business purposes. Formerly a bakery, barber shop and tavern,, the entry was positioned to be equally accessible to customers coming from either Third or Park Streets.

BETHEL METHODIST MEETING HOUSE

214 Mulberry Street(Map #15)

"We have a chapel built in Lewistown," wrote the Bishop of the Methodist Episcopal Church in America when he visited in 1790, looking upon this example of what John Wesley called a 'preaching house'. In 1828 its length was extended by 10 feet to accommodate the growing congregation (20 families), a balcony would subsequently be added for African-Americans who were segregated from their white brethren. When the grand 'new' church (now condominiums) was built on Mulberry Street in 1870, the meeting house was moved for a second time to its present location

Photo provided by Lewes historical Society

THE OLD BLACK SCHOOL HOUSE
(307 SHIPCARPENTER)

The first African arrived in Delaware in 1639, a slave named Black John brought to Fort Christina (Wilmington) from the Caribbean. By the Revolution, there were perhaps a thousand blacks in Sussex County. Slavery persisted in Delaware but failed to flourish. With little cultivation in the state of cotton or tobacco that required year-round tending, farmers found it cheaper to hire free black labor. On the eve of the Civil War 5,700 blacks resided in Sussex County (4,370 of whom were free).

Although Delaware did not secede, its strong Confederate sentiments coalesced in the passage of Jim Crow laws starting in 1876. Miscegenation statutes banned inter-racial marriage; hotels and restaurants and public transportation were segregated; tuberculosis hospitals for whites excluded blacks. Among the Jim Crow Code, which would not be repealed until the late 1960s, were segregated schools with a separate tax on blacks to support black schools (Pierre S. DuPont, opposed to Delaware's segregated system for collecting school taxes, would spend more than $6 million to build 89 schools throughout the state for African-Americans).

BIKE TOURS,
OVER THE BRIDGE TO
ROOSEVELT INLET

NO FISHING,
CRABBING OR
SWIMMING
FROM BRIDGE

The atmosphere of Lewes as a fishing and beach town come alive on this 'wheels tour' to the Roosevelt Inlet. Vestiges of the Lewes that once maintained the country's largest commercial fishing fleets harvesting vast schools of menhaden are rekindled along Fisherman's Wharf. En route to the placid town beach at the end of Savannah Road, one passes beside wetlands that are both stunning and ecologically vital. Just before the Bay, you

the cross-roads intersection of the vintage Dairy Queen and 2 Dips Ice Cream (with the wonderfully eccentric military museum next door).

Beach houses, many passed through multiple generations of the same family, line the streets. The dominant tone is modest and 'old school' although along the waterfront are some grander statements. Roosevelt Inlet, the cut through to the ocean from the canal, makes the point feel like an island. It is a favorite spot for

FROM ST. PETER'S SQUARE GO EAST ON MARKET STREET, THEN HEAD SOUTH ON FRONT STREET

The post office is a grand dowager, very old school and nostalgic. The mostly empty offices upstairs recall Humphrey Bogart private eye movies (or maybe Prairie Home Companion's Guy Noir).

In the next block are some interesting shops. In Sand N Stones you can find sea-glass wrapped into wire-framed jewelry by owner Michele Buckler. Puzzles, a store devoted to jig-saw and cross-word puzzles, celebrated its twentieth anniversary in 2012.

Cross over the Lewes Drawbridge. Make sure to walk your bike. You won't get arrested if you don't, but there may be a few angry glances cast your way. As you cross from the mainland to the beach, look out over the waterway that the original Dutch settlers traveled. Today, it is the canal that connects the Broadkill River (northward) to Rehoboth Bay (southward) but back then it was a creek, populated by flocks of wild swans.

ANGLER'S ROAD

Along Angler's Road, turn left at the foot of the bridge, is Lewes' marina scene. Here's the place to savor a seafarer's lifestyle amidst the docks and boatyards. 'Tiderunners Bait & Tackle' shop supplies fishing licenses and free advice! Along Fisherman's Wharf, private charter boats are docked and 'walk on' head boats offer fishing and dolphin watching. For those who want their fish served up dock side, there's the Fisherman's Wharf seafood restaurant and Irish Eyes bar and restaurant.

SAVANNAH ROAD TO LEWES BEACH

As you head toward the beach, to your right is an expanse of marshland where one can view a heron or egret standing sentry ready to pounce in the watery fields. To the left you'll pass by the Beacon Hotel, The Peninsula Gallery of art, and the town's resident bike shop.

Before the crossroad leading to Cape Henlopen State Park, is the closest thing to a boardwalk in town. Just at the convergence of Two Scoops Ice Cream (try cappuccino crunch), and a vintage Dairy Queen (whose opening in March marks the beginning of summer). Adjoining 2 Dips is a one-of-a-kind museum displaying its owner's lifelong collection of 'things' ranging from military uniforms to vintage license plates.

Lewes Town Beach (not to be confused with the ocean beaches at Cape Henlopen) is located at the end of Savannah Road and looking onto the Delaware Bay, where the water is usually warmer, the sand is cleaner, the crowds are thinner and the setting more mellow (read: ideal for toddlers). You won't find substantial waves here, but there's also little need to be on the lookout for, as one social networker puts, 'weirdo's and riff-raff.' Another frequent visitor calls it "a small gem of a summer playground."

BAY AVENUE

Bay Avenue is a mecca of 'old school' beach life, a family friendly neighborhood, with no bars or nightlife. You might spot one or two McMansions nestled against the dunes built with an eye to weekly in-season rentals, but most of the houses here were built to be enjoyed rather than for show. For a glimpse of 'stylish Lewes hipster-funk', check out the brightly-colored Blue Water House Bed & Breakfast (407 E. Market St.), a primo destination for an off-the-beaten-track getaway.

At 1800 Bay Avenue is The Children's Beach House, founded in 1936 by Lydia Chichester DuPont for handicapped children, especially those stricken with polio. "One of my vivid memories,' a 1950's resident recalled, "is seeing boys and girls who were exactly my age, trying to walk down to the beach in metal leg braces, on crutches, or being carried or pulled in wag-

ons-all because of polio." To this day, The Children's Beach House mission remains loyal to Miss Lydia's vision of helping at-risk and special needs children experience the same healing qualities of the coastal environment that she herself had found.

The Lewes Yacht Club (2701 Cedar Street), situated at the end of Lewes Beach and the mouth of the Delaware Bay, was organized in the early 1930s (Dues: $3, Initiation: $1). The marina facility, refurbished at a cost of more than one million dollars in 2009, is open to the boating public for the sale of gasoline and ice.

Photo provided by Lewes historical Society

Public Commons Beachland

The Lewes beachfront, all the way west to the canal, is almost entirely common land, collectively owned by the town in a most unique historical heritage of a public trust. Property, with rare exception, in the 130-plus acres below the Draw Bridge is held through long-term 99 year leaseholds and not by private title.

This practice dates back to the beginning of the settlement.

Early inhabitants of Delaware and Pennsylvania felt they were entitled to all marsh lands as communal pasture by virtue of unwritten law, 'woods to be common for food for cattle and firewood.' The principle would be tested often into the twentieth century but generations of judges consistently concurred with the spirit of the 1682 grant that ceded '...the land of the Cape commonly called Cape Inlopen laying on the North East side of the Creek formerly called the Whorekill...belong be and forever hereafter Lye in Common for the use of the Inhabitants of the Town of Lewes (sic)...to fish get and take care of there oyster & cockle shells and gather plums, cranberrys and Huckleberrys.' ■

ROOSEVELT INLET

The Roosevelt Inlet lies at the southern edge of the Delaware Bay, linking the Lewes and Rehoboth Canal to the ocean via Cape Henlopen, which lies three nautical miles to the west. Mud, clay, and sand were dredged across the barrier beach, beginning in 1936, followed by the installation of steel sheet-piling jetties to stabilize the waterway. As with most tidal inlets along sandy coastlines, the presence of the inlet has resulted in significant erosion experienced by the adjacent beaches.

In the fall of 2004, a dredge struck an 18th-century wreck site during beach replenishment, resulting in thousands of artifacts being scattered along Lewes Beach. These were the remains of the cargo ship Severn, returning from Bristol, England in 1774 to its home port of Philadelphia loaded with household items and building supplies for the colonial market when it encountered a nor'easter and ran aground.

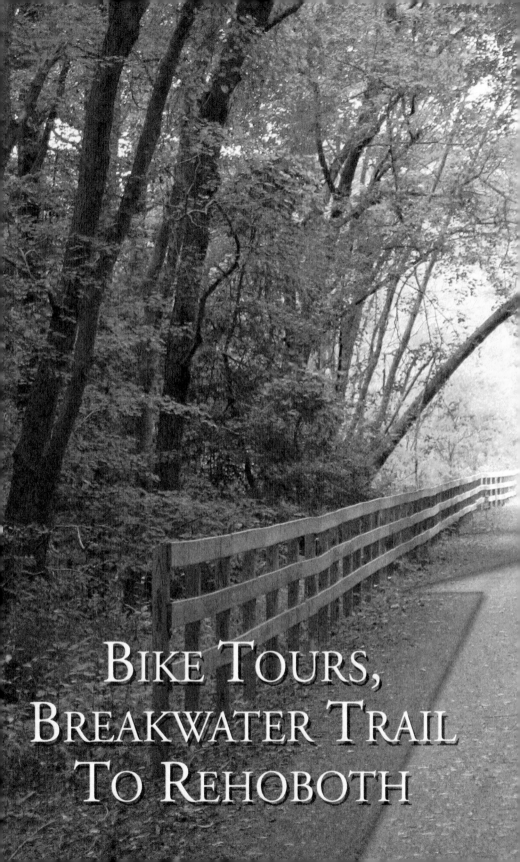

Bike Tours, Breakwater Trail To Rehoboth

THE MYSTICAL SPLENDOR OF COASTAL FOREST

For a journey of serenity, seekers of seaside solace should make time to experience the Junction and Breakwater Trail.

An almost 6-mile trail runs between Lewes and Rehoboth following 19th century rail lines from one seaside town to the next. Today, following the trail provides an opportunity to escape traffic and savor the best of "slower lower" Delaware with vistas of the wetlands, farmlands and forests that natives call home.

The simplest way to reach the Trail from town is to head south on Gills Neck Road. Split rail fencing borders the path until signs direct users inside the community of Hawkseye, where a paved corridor in the median of Golden Eagle Boulevard is a threshold to forested portions of the trail.

At the end of the corridor, turning on a pine-needle pathway sheltered by the trail oak, hemlock and maple tree canopy brings travelers into the mystical splendor of coastal forest. An oasis from the hot sun, crowded beaches and bustling down-town marketplace, a trip to the Breakwater Trail will soon shift an overheated, sunburned vacation nightmare into a midsummer night's dream.

Other joggers, bikers and strolling sight-seers who are privy to the best-kept secret of the Cape Region pepper the pathway, reminding the more leisurely to stay to the right so they can pass (the trail is also prime training ground for distance runners). The suburban sound of lawnmowers is soon replaced by the tenor of gravel crunching beneath bike tires, birds singing and gears shifting. The first of two bridges takes hikers over the marshes at Wolfe Glade with views of the wetlands, which play an important role in maintaining the health of marine ecosystems.

Shortly thereafter, the trail crosses Wolfe Neck Road, where a nearby trailhead feeds into the main route. At the trailhead, a parking lot, restrooms, sycamore trees, picnic tables and benches frame the cypress-shingled Wolfe House, an old farmhouse (circa 1875) that is a restoration work-in-progress.

The trail continues until one side of trees becomes farmland where rows of corn silk in summer. When the sunshine has softened, the heat has subsided and the fireflies begin to glow, deer are oftentimes dining in these fields.

As the trail begins to break into short sections closer to Rehoboth Beach, signs and mile markers keep users informed of how far they've come. At the first fork, a left turn leads trail users around more farmland and behind Little League fields, finally emerging on Holland Glade Road, where it's possible to reach Rehoboth Beach on pavement.

At the second fork, continuing straight will yield still more wooded trail that opens to farmlands and a quick return to reality facing the rear end of the Seaside Outlets Center (many users begin their journey at this spot, making use of the parking lot behind the outlets as an alternate trailhead).

But bearing left at that fork provides yet another path, across Holland Glade Road to a final wooded segment of trail to the Rehoboth trailhead at Hebron Road. Despite the surrounding 360 degree hum of humanity, these woods still stay enchantingly quiet. It's like hiding in plain sight, easy to imagine Puck perched in a tree high above, plotting mischief and timing the drop of an acorn to coincide with the passage of an unsuspecting pate.

Reaching the end of the trail at Hebron Road, some will chose to continue their workout with a U-turn back the way they came, but the alternate option is to check out Rehoboth Beach. Signage directs users to the intersection of Church Street and Rehoboth Avenue, where a left turn leads 'downtown' to the ocean.

For the sight-seeing trail blazer with an appetite, Green Man, a restaurant and juice bar on the first block of Wilmington Avenue, supplies a serious selection of healthful options to recharge batteries. Another option is Arena's Deli, which is located on the block of Rehoboth

Avenue between First and Second Streets in a throughway called Village by the Sea. This relaxed sandwich shop provides the opportunity to filter in with locals, grab a bite to eat, catch the game and maybe crack open a craft brew.

The Junction and Breakwater Trail – in a semi-permanent state of expansion since it opened in 2003 – will one day link with other railways-turned-nature trails across the state with the promise of creating a complete pedestrian-bicycle byway at least as far as Georgetown. Most of us can barely wait. ■

By Molly MacMillan
Molly MacMillan is a freelance journalist who has lived near Lewes most of her life.

BIKE TOURS,
UP THE CANAL

From St. Peter's Square, head on Market Street toward the Inn at Canal Square, the town's Nantucket-style landmark, then bearing left (north) on Pilottown Road for a breezy view of the arts, history, ecology, technology, maritime heritage and small-town appeal that make Lewes so special.

Canalfront Park is usually alive in fair weather with activities, onlookers and even

provide a venue for kayakers and paddle boarders to launch into the canal. Baseball has been a big thing in Lewes since the 19th century, that small-town spirit is preserved in the Little League stadium (opening day in April is marked by a downtown parade, all the more celebratory because Lewes was Delaware District 3 champ in 2012). Small-town Americana at its best!

THE OVERFALLS LIGHT SHIP

The Overfalls Light Ship, moored in its own slip at 219 Pilottown Road adjacent to Canalfront Park, is one of barely more than a dozen surviving lightships of the 179 that were built from 1820-1952. Lightships came of age in the 19th century when they were moored over treacherous reefs or to mark the narrow approaches to a channel or harbor where lighthouses could not be built.

The Overfalls light produced 15,000 lumens of candlepower visible for 13 miles on a clear night. Its foghorn had an audible range of five miles.

She was decommissioned in 1972 following stationing off Old Saybrook, Connecticut, Martha's Vineyard, and Boston Harbor.

Donated by the Coast Guard to the Lewes Historical Society for $1, she was renamed Overfalls, in recognition of the lightship station that designated the Overfalls Shoals at the entrance to Delaware Bay from 1898 until 1960. Overfalls is a marine terms for "under-water waterfall," a natural phenomenon that occurs when fast moving tidal currents flow over a steep drop of underwater sand deposits, thereby creating turbulence on the surface.

A comprehensive development plan began in 1999, which included towing the ship to Norfolk, Virginia for extensive repairs and repainting. More than $1.2 million has been raised over the years through the efforts of the Overfalls Foundation. In 2011 she was designated a National Historic Landmark.

Tours of the ship are regularly offered from Memorial Day through Columbus Day on Mondays, Thursdays, Fridays and Saturdays from 10:00 AM through 4:00 PM and on Sunday from 12:00 through 4:00.

The Lewes Life-Saving Station (behind the stadium on the Canal) was established in 1884 and proved its worth in the Great Blizzard of 1888 which left hundreds of frozen sailors clinging to icy masts behind the breakwall, requiring rescue throughout the night. It responded to more than three dozen shipwrecks during its commission. Surfboats and life saving equipment are displayed inside.

Past the Little League fields, the landscape transforms into boat boathouses and slips lining the canal. Even though Lewes is bicycle-friendly, many drivers may be unsteady in the transport of their sea-craft along Pilottown Road and take more of the roadway than they realize. So ride carefully!

THOMAS MAULL HOUSE (542 Pilottown Road)

It is hard from the outside to gauge the age of old houses in Lewes, where unpainted sheathing soon takes on the appearance of age from wind and rain. In this case, the house was built around 1750.

Maull house one hosted Jerome Bonaparte, Napoleon's brother, and his new bride Betsey Patterson of Baltimore on a stormy night in 1803 when their ship bound for France had to put in to Lewes. They were taken here for shelter. But Betsey refused to sit down to the bounteous supper of roast goose prepared in their honor until a messenger was dispatched back to the ship to fetch her silver candlesticks.

BLACK HARRY'S SPRING

Be on the lookout for Black Harry's Spring (at Queen Anne Road, on the Canal side). It's easy to miss but rich in significance as the gathering spot in 1784 to hear one of early Methodism's great itinerant preachers. Born a North Carolina slave, Harry 'Hosier' ('hosier' was rural Southern slang time for 'bumpkin') was freed after the American Revolution and became a legendary travelling preacher. "There is such an amazing power attends his preaching, though he cannot read," observed America's Methodist Bishop at the time. His passion transcended the racial barriers of his time as he was the first black man to preach from a Delaware church pulpit.

'YE OLD FOUNTAIN OF YOUTH'

Several hundred yards past the intersection of New Road/Route 266, you'll see the 'Ye Olde Fountain of Youth.' 17th century explorers took the prospects seriously that there was a magical elixir to be found in the New World. Even as Ponce de Leon set out to locate it in Florida, Dutch settlers thought they'd already found the fountain of youth here. The Chamber of Commerce, alert to the marketing potential of a good thing, erected the memorial gazebo in 1937 although the well itself is now dry.

LEWES DAIRY

The Lewes Dairy shipping facility is at 660 Pilottown. For much of the 20th century, the Brittingham family owned lands at the northern end of Lewes where they operated a dairy farm, selling their own and locally-farmed milk throughout Delmarva as Lewes Dairy product. It was long celebrated for the fresh, heavy cream that was sought by chefs as far away as Washington, D.C. Its egg nog, bottled between Thanksgiving and New Years, remains a much awaited holiday treat. Lewes Dairy merged with Hy-Point Dairy of Wilmington in 2011.

Before the road ends at the public boat ramp and inlet, bicyclists pass two cemeteries on the left. The first and oldest is an old African Methodist Episcopal cemetery just before the Pilottown Park development. This cemetery not only features two of the largest hackleberry trees in Delaware, but the grave sites of three colored soldiers who fought in the Civil War—the only federal gravestones in Lewes. The second cemetery is located just in front of the University of Delaware College of Earth and Marine Studies.

UNIVERSITY OF DELAWARE

Explore the campus of the University of Delaware College of Earth, Ocean and Environment.

Exhibits on the first floor of the Harry L. Cannon Laboratory (the first building) offer an introduction to the range of remarkable research being conducted here. There are simple but illuminating displays about hydrothermal vents in the ocean floor (deep sea organisms living here may well be descendants of the oldest life on earth), horseshoe crabs, Right Whales, and a model of the research ship Hugh R. Sharp. There are also two aquariums of local fish, one devoted to the rocky tidal habitat of the Lewes harbor breakwaters and the other to marsh habitat ("salt marshes rank with coral reefs and mangrove forests as the most productive of all coastal habitats").

Ride past the buildings along a pathway leading to the wind turbine, which towers above the horizon and grows ever taller as you approach.

WIND TURBINE

The sun heats the earth at different rates at different times, the variance in temperature generates pressure disparities that drive the movement of air and—presto---it creates kinetic energy that can be harnessed into electricity. Which is what the 256-foot tall wind turbine does.

The rotating blades driven by the wind create mechanical energy that turns a generator that makes enough electricity to power 500 homes a year or, in this case, the six buildings of the University of Delaware campus (with any surplus sold to Lewes).

It has been operational since 2010.

If the blades aren't spinning, it's probably because there's not enough wind (required minimum is 8 miles per hour) although another reason might be that researchers are studying the effect of the turbine on bats and birds.

CAPE HENLOPEN STATE PARK

Cape Henlopen State Park is a vast reserve of over 5,000 acres that spans six miles of undeveloped beach front, rolling dunes, camp grounds, a 24-hour fishing pier, a nature center with aquariums and exhibits, the Biden Environmental Training Center, one of the most heavily armored coastal fortresses ever built, and miles of hiking and biking trails.

The Park falls at the juncture of two ecological habitats, the farthest south for northern species (like pitch pines) and the farthest north for southern (big glossy dark-leaved magnolias). "The poor man's Galapagos," is how one park naturalist describes Henlopen's remarkably varied niche.

The daily entry fee is $4 for Delaware residents, $8 for out-of-state. Annual passes are $27 for state-registered vehicles, $54 for out-of-state ($12 and $24 respectively for seniors).

A BOG WALK IN EARLY SPRING

Early one Saturday morning, in the cold March light, I set out for the winter Bog Walk at Cape Henlopen State Park. I was wearing sneakers rather than boots because I had been told that Henlopen's bogs are generally higher and drier than lowland bogs due to their location above the Park's shoreline.

Our tour guide, Lauren Barbieri, a Park Naturalist, gathered us in the Fort Miles parking lot on the leeward side of the Great Dune, to begin our descent along a well-marked trail into the bog lands. She cautioned us to stay within the trail markers as the extreme conditions of salt water, and wind makes this a very fragile environment. Fragile, indeed, but at the same time these conditions have created a specific ecological niche for many hardy species that have adapted to this unforgiving environment.

Under a thick grove of pine, light filtering through the canopy, it was easy even to my untrained eye to spot different types of trees. Lauren told us that some of these were native (like the pitch and lob lolly) and one imported (the Japanese black pine, planted for soil stabilization which is an on-going problem given the shifting nature of the dune)..

We got a quick lesson in how to tell which is which. Lauren tweezed a small hank of needles from a branch and separated out a stalk to show three needles attached to a single bud end. By their length (shorter than 5") and the fact that they grew directly out of the trunk (like the whiskers on an old Salt's chin), this was a native pitch pine. The less common southern lob lolly grows much straighter (which is why it was favored for the tall masts and yardarms used in the colonial shipyards), throwing out at its height a defining crown of branches. Two needles joined in the shape of a "V" make for a neat mnemonic device to spot Virginia pines.

Cape Henlopen marks where the habitat ranges of northern and southern pines overlap. Other species here have similarly breached this porous line of demarcation. A growing numbers of snow geese now winter on our local corn fields instead of migrating southward; fishermen report catches of Florida pompano and subtropical pinfish swimming off our coast.

Lauren led our search for the 'star attraction' of Cape Henlopen, its native cranberry bogs (although for those thinking of Cape Cod, 'bog' may be a stretch). They are native to this sandy soil, which has an acidic pH level due to the carpet of pine needles decaying in freshwater pools left by winter storms. Henlopen's cranberry plants, low-lying and vine-like, are hard to spot. This March day, they displayed small round, green and red winter leaves with an occasional berry left over from the summer.

In spring, these bushes will grow delicate white flowers in the shape of a Crane's head---hence the origins of their name, the "Crane berry". Within each seedling is a tiny air bubble, which makes commercial harvesting easy because the berry floats to the surface when the bog is flooded. Like everything else in this isolated wind-swept environment, these plants have had to be tough to survive.

As we approached the summit of the Great Dune, trees began to shrink in size. Limbs exposed to the seaward side were stunted, withered from the wind and salt spray known as "salt shear."

Lauren pointed out clumps of beach heather that grow low to the ground like the cranberry but sprout a tiny yellow flower. Nearby were small pale green-bluish lichens (composite organisms of a fungus and photosynthetic partner growing together in a symbiotic relationship). Darker green mosses growing in thick clumps cushioned our feet.

A little girl in our group shouted with glee, she had found a long whitened bone at the side of the trail. "Most likely a humerus from the leg of a small deer," said Lauren. Fresh tracks could be seen. Cape Henlopen has grown a large deer population due to the lack of natural predators (although coyotes have been on the outskirts of Lewes). Hunters are allowed to cull the herd annually in certain parts of the park to reduce this environmental stressor.

Further along the trail, I found a partial fur-covered skull from a red fox. Lauren explained that there are two types of foxes in the park, the endangered native grey fox and the imported red fox which came over with the first British colonials for their fox hunts. A number of these, however, eluded their pursuers and now, several centuries later, are sufficiently abundant to cause dismay for local "free range" chicken farmers.

We had returned to where we began. Without Lauren's guidance, this easily could have been an uneventful walk through an undistinguished landscape. Through her eyes, though, we were filled with a wonder for the fine calibrations of natural balance that surrounded us. ∎

By Rob Sturgeon
Photographs by Lauren Barbieri

The Pitch Pine

The ubiquitous pitch pines in the Park are the only strand to be found on the Delmarva Peninsula. They are most easily identified by their distinctive three twisted needle clusters and by sprouts emerging from up the trunk.

The species takes it name from the comparatively large amount of resin sap in its wood, enabling it to resist decay (and making it great for kindling a campfire). This resiliency made its timber ideal for ship masts, railroad ties, and mine supports.

These pines establish their niche in shallow, gravelly soil that most flora find inhospitable. The sandy outwash glacial plain of Cape Henlopen, for example, is ideal.

The pitch pine has a remarkable capability to survive adversity, particularly forest fires due to its thick bark. Even if the entire stem is killed, say by deer clipping a seedling down to an inch or two, the tree can re-sprout by sending out shoots.

Although not as fast growing as other eastern conifers, pitch pines often live 200 years.

FORT MILES
AMERICA'S FIRST TRUE HOMELAND SECURITY

Fort Miles, one of the largest and most heavily armed coastal fortifications ever built, went operational in 1941 (four days before Pearl Harbor) on a reservation of some 2,000 acres (543 of which were returned to the state of Delaware in 1964, forming the heart of Cape Henlopen Park). The 2,200 men stationed here during World War II made it larger than the town of Lewes at the time.

The Fort was named after Nelson Appleton Miles, a Massachusetts farm boy who volunteered in the Union army in 1861 and ended his career some forty years later as the Army's Commanding General, its highest ranking officer. A strikingly handsome, imposing man (Theodore Roosevelt described him as "a proud peacock"), Miles died at the age of 85 while attending the circus with his grandchildren and is buried in one of only two mausoleums at Arlington National Cemetery.

The mission of Fort Miles was to defend assets along the Delaware River and Bay from attack---Philadelphia's oil refineries and Naval Shipyard, the major industrial center of Trenton, DuPont's munitions and nylon factories. A secondary mission was to protect domestic shipping from U-boat submarines.

Although largely kept from the public because of news embargo, the Germans torpedoed and sank 14 ships off New Jersey in the first six months of 1942 alone. "You could stand out here on top of the Great Dune and at night see shipping on fire," reported one observer.

Installations, with guns varying in size from 3 inches to 16 inches and a range as far as 25 miles, consisted of Battery 519 (the current site of historical Fort Miles, open to visitors) as well as batteries mounted near Point Comfort and Herring Point.

Eleven 80-foot-tall "fire control towers" stretched along the Delaware and New Jersey coastline with a sight range of almost 15 miles out to sea. When two towers sighted the same target, its coordinates could be triangulated providing aim for the gunners. Five of the towers continue to loom above the Henlopen landscape, one of which (#7) is open to visitors eager to navigate the circular staircase to the top.

The guns of Fort Miles never fired in combat during the war (although a German submarine did surrender here after the armistice). By 1948 most of the installations were decommissioned, the only one bunker left in operation was a top secret listening unit for Soviet subs that operated until1981.

The Fort Miles Historic Area grounds, atop the Great Dune consisting of various battery exhibits and buildings, are open 8 a.m. to sunset. The Orientation Building is open 10 a.m. to 4 p.m. Tuesday through Saturday from April 1 through October 30. Public access to the underground bunker of Battery 519 is only through guided tours or private bookings (302) 645-6852. ∎

WES DINING SCE
FRESH TO THE TABLE

The fundamentals of good food, newly picked produce and shly caught fish, abound in wes. The Cape may not ve bragging rights amongst odies but it's their loss. The of the farm to table move-

ment, with its emphasis le on gastronomic razzle-dazz and more on local tomatoe bodes well for Lewes' reputa tion. The wave of chef-owne restaurants opened in the pa half-dozen years is makin good on that

CONVERSATION: MATT HALEY
Owner of Fish On! and SoDel Concepts

FISH, TOMATOES, AND CORN!
THAT'S WHAT I RECOMMEND TO EAT IN LEWES.

Many of the best moments in Matt Haley's turbulent youth were spent making meals with his mother. His route to the restaurant trade may have been convoluted, but his food roots go deep. From the opening of Fish On! Seafood Bar and Grill in Lewes (Village of Five Points) in 2005, SoDel Concepts has grown into the biggest restaurant operation in Delaware. In 2012, the Lewes-Cape May Ferry and terminal was added to their roster.

In addition to running restaurants, Haley is an engaged public citizen who started the Global Delaware Fund *to support children in Nepal, and is the President of the Board of* L'Esperanza, *a non-profit dedicated to providing social services to the lower Delaware Hispanic population.*

There's all kinds of good eating fish here, some that you might not think of. It's illegal to buy straight off the boats, the fish has to go through a licensed dealer, but you can certainly catch your own. Take Croaker, they're easy to catch at the inlet. Some call it 'trash fish' but it's tasty. Or skate. Lots of people don't know that there are scallops in the Bay, you can get them alive and fresh in the shell. Sea trout, too.

Monk fish is found here, mostly in the fall and spring. One of the best things you can eat is monk fish liver, in Japan it's a delicacy that they're getting from the Atlantic. Pan sear it with grape seed oil, finish with sherry vinegar and butter, maybe pour capers over it. It's the foie gras of the sea. Awesome!

Halibut starts running in spring. Tuna's here, fifty miles off-shore. You can look at a piece of tuna and tell where it's from and what it's been eating. Dark red tuna has been moving fast, pumping blood, and eating mullet which helps for the coloring and flavor. When it's lighter and pinker it's been slowing down and eating squid.

Wolf fish is something you won't often find but it's phenomenal. It's a bottom feeder with big teeth and a strong jaw, looks like a wolf. It feeds off shell fish. Clams and oysters and even lobsters. The meat is pure white, like chalk and so flavorful---you can tell that it's been eating well.

Much of the local fish gets pushed up to Philadelphia or Jessup, Md. and then gets turned around and comes back down here. The place to get anything is Lewes Fish House, Chuck Donahue is the best in the business (17696 Coastal Highway, 302-644-0708).

Corn is great, it makes the world go round. In Delaware it's a staple. Bringing out the best in corn is so simple, just butter and salt (although I prefer Old Bay seasoning). We do a white peach or white nectarine and corn salad that is great (the season for white peaches is only about three weeks long, starting at the end of July): take the corn off the cob, shave the peach or nectarine, and mix it with fresh lemon or olive oil and, if you're daring, fresh chili. Mix crab in it, too.

When it comes to tomatoes, New Jersey and Delaware are two of the best places in the world to grow them. If you really want to 'bite into Delaware,' go pick a tomato at 2:00 in the afternoon after it's been sitting in the hot sun that has brought out all the sugar. My favorite way to eat tomato is to put it on a slice of Wonderbread with Hellman's mayonnaise, that's the sandwich I grew up with. ∎

BAKED WHITE FISH, 'FARM-STAND SAUTE', WATERMELON

"Get some flounder or fluke, sauté it and finish with Old Bay and butter. Go to the farmer's market or a road stand and buy one of everything: eggplant, zucchini , squash, tomato, corn, garlic, soy beans, onion. Dice it all up. You've got to put the tomatoes in the pan first, cook them down so you don't get soup. Then add the zucchini and squash. Then the rest, with the eggplant last since it cooks the fastest and you don't want it to fall apart but rather to absorb the tomato flavor. Finish with a pour of extra virgin olive oil and cool to room temperature. That's what we call 'Delaware ratatouille.'"

THE LEWES RESTAURANT SCENE

The opening of the Buttery in 1994, at the north end of Second Street where the Rose and Crown now stands, marked the coming of foodies to Lewes. In a town that was hardly known for its restaurants, the vision of owner John Donato was as unlikely as it was ambitious: a Paris bistro (complete with its own charcuterie) on the eastern shore. Some twenty years later, its location now a lovingly restored Victorian Mansion, the Buttery continues to set a standard for fine dining.

Lisa McDonald has been the manager and 'guiding presence' at The Buttery for the past half-dozen years. Her rise as a restaurateur was unintended. She had planned to be an attorney until a law-school internship at a Washington firm soured her on the lawyer life style. She retreated to her aunt's condo in Lewes and ended up buying "a local greasy spoon" in 1998. "It was great. I was feeding the cops and firemen and the public works guys and the water-men (fishing was still good). Slinging eggs in the morning was about as far away as I could get from my previous life."

There's some very good restaurants here. You can come to town without a reservation and find a good place to eat dinner. It's good for all of us that Lewes is getting known as a food destination in its own right, not just a side-trip from Rehoboth.

Everybody here is going to do a crab cake. That's what people from metro centers expect when they come to the beach. We change our menu four times a year with the seasons and have done so for 17 years, but the one thing that never changes is the crab cake. At the Buttery it's essentially all crab, there's almost no filler. Just the tiniest amount of egg and mixture so it won't fall apart. 99 times out of 100 it gets a rave review, but when a customer complains, it's usually that they don't really like crab, they're looking for a deep fried something-or-other.

I feel like a 'back to basics' reaction is starting to build. That doesn't mean 'dumbing down' the food but I suspect those of us in the restaurant business are going to start taking ourselves a little less seriously. We've always been conservative at The Buttery, we don't want to be 'edgy' but we are trying to be more 'playful.' My goal isn't to dazzle customers with complicated dishes but rather, as a composed plate restaurant, 'wow' them with the quality of the ingredients and perfection of the preparation.

People come to the coast and they want to eat seafood. That's only natural. But the truth is that all the restaurants are getting their fish from the same source and the catch isn't local. My favorite dish on our menu is the chicken. The chickens we serve eat better than I do, they're from a farm six miles away in Milton. They're absolutely delicious. But when you're on vacation at the seashore at a 'special occasion' restaurant like the Buttery, you're not thinking chicken.

With deserts it's the same thing, we're sticking to basics but with a new spin on old favorites dressed up for the grown-up palate. We're going to do individualized fruit pies in season, they'll be juicier and more flavorful than your traditional slice from a whole pie. Same with individualized cheesecakes. ∎

IT'S NOT LIKE YOU HAVE TO ORDER CRAB CAKES IN LEWES BECAUSE THERE'S NOTHING ELSE

Ian Crandall's mother owned boutique wine shops so he got a taste for great meals when he was growing up. He started out in the wine business himself, but soon discovered "sales wasn't for me." His love for restaurants remained, however, and he entered the trade through the kitchen door as a cook, studying classic French techniques that continue to influence his style.

He and his wife, a pastry chef, cooked in Washington for a number of years and then opted for a different life style. They bought a house in Lewes, started Half Full and eventually opened Kindle in Lewes.

Lewes has always been influenced more by the -northeast than other local beach towns, which are influenced by Baltimore with its crab cakes and Old Bay seasoning. We were a fishing village for a long time, our roots are like New England roots. Fish stews are popular here, as are shellfish and tomatoes.

There's remarkable variety for a town this size. It's not like you have to order crab cakes when you come to Lewes because there's nothing else.

There's a glut of produce here. You can get anything you want. Asparagus grow very well, in late spring we put them into everything. In summer, there's a certain variety of corn at farm stands, silver queen, that's very, very sweet. I'll get the weirdest stuff that comes from the Farmer's Market like garlic scapes, the curling green tops of garlic plants that are edible.

The heirloom tomato craze is still in full-swing. I like to take smaller, sweet tomatoes and roast them. Put them on anything and it's wonderful. In summer, I'll grill a heartier fish like a maui maui and serve it with roast tomatoes drizzled with olive oil, salt, pepper and fresh basil.

Beets are very popular here, it's a trend a lot of people have jumped on. In spring and summer, you can get locally grown baby beets. There are heirlooms that look like starburst candy with red and white stripes. They are so tender I barely cook them, just give them a blanche and put them in a salad.

Scrapple is a big deal, especially Milton scrapple. You can get it at Lloyds Market, right past the Dairy case. It's fine minced pork meat and other parts with corn meal that's steamed into a loaf that you slice and pan-fry. Scrapple has a lot of history. It's one of those things that farmers around here made and got known for. ■

INSIDER SPECIALTIES OF THE HOUSE

Amber Caramel and Harvest Hazelnut at Kings Ice Cream

Local ice creamery of note teams up with 16 Mile (local brewery of note) to bring you two delicious treats. Remember malted milk? These delights are made with the malty brew used to make 16 Mile's Amber Sun and Harvest Ales. No alcohol, of course, but just as memorable.

The Kobe Burger at The Buttery Pub

Lewes' best-kept secrets are the happy hour bar noshes at the Buttery. This upscale dining icon puts out a wallet-friendly menu for afternoon sippers in their dark and cozy drinkery. The richly delicious Kobe burger fits right in with the classic ambiance of The Buttery.

Homemade mozzarella at Touch of Italy

A little bit of the Bronx (Arthur Avenue, to be exact) sits at the corner of Second and Savannah. Mozzarella maven Mikey Berardinelli oversees the creation of each and every milky, snow white orb. Bring a cooler: You'll want to take some home.

Fried oysters at Jerry's Seafood

For those who believe seafood was put on this Earth to be fried, Jerry's does it right! Also try the fish & chips. Both share a crunchy crust that's light and tasty. Frying is an art – sample the artwork at Jerry's.

Short Rib Sliders at Rose & Crown

Beef short ribs are braised in local beer and then topped with melted gruyere. This meal-in-itself starter, created by James Beard-nominated chef Jay Caputo, is not to be missed.

Crab Cakes at Gilligan's

Chef/owner Cheryl Tilton is so proud of these flaky orbs that she named them after herself. Cheryl's Crab Cake is about 99.9% tender, white crabmeat. Add that to the view of the harbor, and you have the perfect Lewes bite.

Classic Soft-Serve at Dairy Queen

What trip to the beach is complete without elbowing your way to the window for a creamy cone and then strolling along Lewes Beach at sunset? It's might even drip down onto your hand, but that's part of the experience. Don't mess with tradition!

Upscale Chocolate Truffles at Edie Bee's

Edie Bee's is not your average candy store. Yes, they have all the vintage sweets, including fruit slices, gummy everythings and a whole shelf with nothing but licorice, but they also feature top-notch confections including handmade love bugs and bees from Philly-based John & Kira's Chocolates. Cute and worth every penny.

The Ooey Gooey from the Lewes Bake Shoppe/Notting Hill Roastery

Some may call it a twist. Others insist it's a danish. Yet others call it a sticky bun. In fact, the Ooey Gooey at Lewes Bake Shoppe is all of those things. This is a knife and fork event if there ever was one. If you try to pick it up, you'll know why they named it what they did. Enjoy it with freshly roasted coffee.

By The Rehoboth Foodie
The Rehoboth Foodie is the author of the popular travel app, **Rehoboth In My Pocket,** *now available for iPhone, iPad and Android devices.*

HISTORIC LEWES FARMERS MARKET
THE FRESHEST LOCAL FOOD AVAILABLE

The Historic Lewes Farmers Market, ranked among 'America's Favorite' in its size class by the American Farmland Trust, is a community-based producer-only market. It is part of a growing environmental movement committed to save the land, provide small farmers and producers a way to stay in business, and educate children (and their parents) about the food we eat.

Opened in 2006, the market takes place on the grassy grounds of the Historic Society (with the exception of the weeks when the Craft Show and Sea Glass Show take over the venue and the market moves to the Shields School Parking Lot, 910 Shields Avenue at Savannah Highway).

In addition to 'just-picked' seasonal produce, there are eggs (duck as well as chicken), artisan cheeses, milk and dairy (the yogurt goes fast, the whole milk is so delicious you'll abandon skim), free-range lamb and meat and chicken, bread and baked goods, Bay oysters and crab, cut-flowers, herbs and even lavender potpourri.

Cooking demonstrations are given each week (with free tastings afterwards), often by chefs from area restaurants. A story hour takes place in the one-room schoolhouse. The celebrated Tomato Festival occurs in mid-August, at the height of the harvest, offering an abundance of Delmarva varieties and heirlooms to sample as well as contests for tomato-based appetizers, soups, entrees, and deserts.

Dogs on leashes used to be welcome until there was one-too-many barking standoff, so no pets allowed. ∎

Saturday mornings, 8 a.m. to noon,
May through September
Lewes Historical Society Grounds
(unless otherwise noted)

THE MAKING OF A FARMER'S MARKET

I had been coming to Lewes for years and always liked shopping at farm stands on the way from Washington. I noticed that I was seeing fewer stands, and more of what was being sold like oranges and grapefruits weren't grown locally.

I met Hattie Allen (of Hatties's Garden), she has a gorgeous acre farm on the outskirts of Lewes, and she told me there was nowhere around here where she could sell her produce. That got me to thinking about starting a market. There was lots of enthusiasm for the idea.

Because I'm a small business/entrepreneur person, I began researching, benchmarking best markets, and talking to other market managers around the country. One of the big things we wanted was to support small farmers. We also wanted to make it a 'producers-only' market, which means that the stands sell only what they themselves grow or make.

We are a non-profit, working on an interesting model. Many markets charge a fixed fee per table per day, but that works to the disadvantage of smaller operations (most of our farms are around 50 acres, although we have one that is 200 acres and several smaller than 10). Instead, in order to give back sufficient margin to the farmers and have farmers of different scale, we charge five percent of sales.

In our plan, we made a list of the attributes that make for a successful market: a central location, shade, running water, bathrooms, a demonstration kitchen. The Lewes Historical Society was perfect and they were very receptive (we pay a weekly rent, which changes yearly). The City Council had to be convinced, there was concern about bothering the neighbors, traffic and noise (that's why we don't have music).

We opened in 2006, in mid-July when we knew we'd have enough vegetables. In the beginning, there were nine vendors: no strawberries, no apple growers, no meat, no fish.

On a busy day—the 4th of July or the Tomato Festival or a beautiful day in mid-summer—we'll have between 3,000 and 3,500 people. Gross sales in 2012 were $525,000, revenue grows each year but our 5% is used up entirely in publicizing and promoting the market. We always have to raise money.

Our goal is to have diversification of product. At this market, you'll see some people sell lettuce through August; somebody else will sell organic potatoes. I wanted meat but it was hard to find small ranchers who were raising grass-fed beef. We now have enough eggs, there were many times in the past when the supply would run out. Cheeses were also tough to get; it's very hard and expensive to do a creamery.

We have limited space, so we're selective. We want to make this a farmer's market, not a food court. The largest percentage of our stands are selling produce and farm product. We supplement that with a mix of breads and prepared foods. One of our prepared food makers, Magnolia Bread Company, grows its own wheat on a 14th generation Delmarva family farm.

Making a farmers market work is a hard thing to do. We depend on two hundred volunteers. It looks seamless from the outside but behind the scene the logistics are complicated. You need to watch out for a gazillion things: lost children, heat stroke, we used to have to position volunteers in different quadrants to look out for dog problems before we banned dogs altogether last year. Book-keeping is quite complex, the farmers report sales the next day and send in their checks within a week.

We have a gleaning program, where excess food is donated to the Casa San Francisco, a soup kitchen in Milton. And we have a scholarship program for farmers to attend the Pennsylvania Sustainable Agricultural Conference in State College, Pennsylvania; the scholarship is open to any small farmer on the Delmarva. They report back to our farmers on what they learned. ∎

INSIDER'S GUIDE TO LOCAL EATERIES

Agave
137 Second Street
302-645-1232

The 'hot spot' on the Lewes dining scene since its opening several years ago is Agave, a stylized Mexican restaurant that bears scant resemblance to any taco-and-refried beans joint where you've ever eaten.

Key to its instant success was the animated, modernistic dining room (since expanded with the addition of the adjoining storefront) arranged around the hippest bar scene in town (with equally hip margaritas sufficiently potent to summon the designated drivers). There's no reservations so waits can be measured by the hour but few complain once they start eating dishes like 'super nachos', the combination guacamole platter (goat cheese and pine nuts, gala apples, roasted pumpkin seeds), jalapenos stuffed with minced chicken infused with cheese, handmade enchiladas, and dark rich (but not too thick) moule sauce

The Buttery
102 Second Street
302-645-7755

Upscale dining (without the upscale attitude). Co-owner John Donato calls it "accessible elegance." Diners typically call it "stuff people like to eat." The veranda dining area overlooking the busy intersection is prime real estate, closely followed by the cupola-style semi-private haven just off the main dining room.

Dinner is the main event, and this long-time Lewes icon is known for generous portions of creative cuisine. Rack of Lamb, Ricotta Gnudi and Ratatouille are examples of what could appear on their seasonal bill of fare. And there's always superb crab cakes.

The Pub Menu served at the bar is one of Lewes' best-kept 5:00 secrets! Year-round Sunday Brunch starts at 10:30. Lunch every day starting at 11:30. A local favorite? The Buttery Beach with a cup of homemade soup.

Gate House of Lewes
109 W. Market Street
302-313-5912

Gretchen and Chip Gates (with sons Wilson and Taylor, an alumnus of New York's renowned Jean-Georges restaurant) bring over 60 years of combined culinary experience to their bistro-style eatery. Expertly crafted dinner entrées include dry-aged prime beef, almond-crusted duck breast and blackened lamb. The garlic lemon kale salad is a must-get. Classical French techniques are most evident in the sauces.

Lunch is served Friday through Sunday in-season, favorites include the brioche BLT and the duck confit with fig jam and roasted peppers.

The restaurant opened in late spring 2014, so both menus are delicious works-in-progress.

Fish On!
17300 N. Village Main Blvd.
Village of Five Points (2 miles west off Savannah Highway)
302-645-9790

The spot for fresh, simple, and delicious seafood. In the Village of Five Points rather than the Lewes 'main drag' but worth the short drive.

Chef/ owner Matt Haley, along with chef Maurice Catlett, use the best available local ingredients, creating specials that change with the tides. Enjoy the flash fried softshell crabs all summer long. As the chill of autumn starts, sample the different rockfish preparations. Happy hour raw bar with $1 oysters from up-and-down the east coast.

Regardless of the time of year, the shrimp-and-grits and Lewes seafood stew have been local cravings since Fish On opened its doors 10 years ago.

Gilligan's
134 W. Market Street
302-644-7230

It only seems right that this tiny dockside eatery started out as an old fishing boat. Over the years, different structures were added (including a Sussex County chicken house) to make it the Lewes landmark it is today. The dockside dining area with its lively bar is the place for insiders to see and be seen. Gilligan's is Lewes as it was meant to be experienced.

The menu is playful. Smashed Potato Eggrolls share the card with White Crab Tandoori Tarts and Duck Potstickers as appetizers! The setting as much as the food is the draw here.

Chef/owner Cheryl Tilton prides herself on Gilligan's crab cakes, and you'll be hard-pressed to find anything in them other than crab. Tantalizing dishes like Peach-Glazed Salmon and Mediterranean Chicken dominate the dinner menu.

Half Full
113 W. Market Street
302-645-8877

Pizza. Just Pizza. And good pizza, at that. It's the gourmet twists and turns that set this petite (500 sq. ft.!) hangout apart.

Rectangular pies are served on a wooden plank with a daring list of toppings: Caramelized onions, flank steak, Granny Smith apples, Butternut squash crème, smoked gouda and blue cheese, Kalamata olives, Italian parsley, roasted chicken. On and on. Of course, there's always pepperoni, sausage and mushrooms for those who'd rather not think out of the pizza box.

Ordering is basic: Belly up to the window, announce your preference, pay, and sip from the wine-bar selections (modest but consistently satisfying). Half Full is lots of fun, especially on a warm summer night when you can sit outside, nibble, sip and people watch.

Irish Eyes
213 Anglers Road
302-645-6888

No description of Lewes dining would be complete without Irish Eyes. The massive restaurant complex offers what seem to be acres of canal front dining, regularly scheduled live music, and down-to-earth bar food.

Shining stars on Irish Eyes' wallet-friendly menu include Cucumber Bruschetta, Reuben Egg Rolls and of course Irish specialties with-a-twist, including a seafood and a vegetarian Shepherd's Pie along with Beef & Guinness Stew. Crab pretzels, steamed shrimp, big salads and full-on main courses.

Irish Eyes' signature cheesecake was a winner at the Rehoboth Beach Chocolate Festival.

JD'S Cafe on Savannah
329 Savannah Highway
302-644-8400

This little diner used to be a gas station – or a car repair depot. Doesn't really matter, because now it's a restaurant with a family friendly menu offering breakfast, lunch and dinner in an atmosphere of vintage license plates and automobile memorabilia.

There's a selection of 10 (count 'em, 10!) burgers and an array of sandwiches including Texas pulled pork and turkey Reuben. For dinner there's fish & chips or in-house roasted turkey. The entire restaurant has been revamped, with a new menu including Bison from nearby Colvine Farms. Prices remain reasonable, and even the main dishes top-out in the high teens.

Jerry's Seafood
108 Second Street
302-645-6611

Jerry's touts itself the "Home of the Crab Bomb," and this (that's a lot of crabmeat!) behemoth will make any crab lover explode with joy. For those with a slightly smaller appetite (or wallet), the Baby Bomb weighs in at 6 ounces.

One of the high points at Jerry's Seafood is their fried entrées. Fried oysters and fish 'n' chips here are among the best. Crabs make cameo appearances throughout the menu, including the Crab Dip appetizer and the Crab Cake entrée sporting 8 ounces of snow-white meat with virtually no filler.

The raw bar menu is a favorite with happy hour aficionados (specials start at 4 p.m.). Friday and Saturday nights offer live entertainment.

Kindle
111 Bank Street
302-645-7887

Lewes and Kindle share at least one thing in common: They're both delightfully small and crowded. Elbow your way inside, enjoy a relaxed sip on the cobblestone walk bordering historic Bank Street, and prepare yourself for well-prepared American comfort food kicked up a notch or two.

Must-gets include the Kindle Fire Fries (roasted chilies blend with Pecorino Romano – potatoes never had it so good) and the Spiced Roast Chicken (honey and smoked paprika impart a mouthwatering glaze). The flame-seared Kindle Burger, crowned with aromatic Gruyere and applewood-smoked bacon, is anything but downscale. This jam-packed Lewes mainstay rarely disappoints and you can't help but make new friends there on a summer evening.

Rose & Crown
142 Second Street
302-827-4475

James Beard-nominated chef Jay Caputo has resurrected the Rose & Crown adjoining the lobby of the Hotel Rodney (the two spaces now flow into one another so restaurant guests can enjoy the hotel ambiance).

A rustic yet modern design that just begs you to order Fried Pickles, a bowl of 5-Onion Soup, something from 16 Mile Brewery just down the road, or a Bacon Cheeseburger where the bacon is cooked right into the patty. Some claim the fried calamari laced hot with peppers is as good as they've ever tasted. See and be seen at Rose & Crown.

Striper Bites
107 Savannah Highway
302-645-4657

The nautical-themed Striper Bites is a little bit Cape Cod and a little bit Key West. The huge beach-house style building sports a generous dining area plus outdoor under-cover dining for rainy days. The bar is the spot to be, especially on Thursday nights when celebrity bartender Andrew Thomas is pouring. Get ready for his jokes.

Soups, salads, starters and sandwiches dominate the menu, but locals love the seafood, pasta, steaks, chicken and jambalaya. A couple of must-check-outs include the Maine Lobster Roll, Striper's signature Amaretto Chicken, and Fish Tacos. Hungry? Dig into the Nor'easter – crab cakes, scallops and shrimp all together in one place.

Spirit lovers will appreciate Striper Bites' selection of unusual potables, including Blanton's Single-Barrel Bourbon, Casa Noble Anejo Tequila and the 80-proof Pyrat XO Reserve. In spite of all these high-falutin' goodies, Striper Bites is still family friendly.

Touch of Italy
101 Second Street
302-827-2730

Touch of Italy delights with authentic Italian meats and cheeses, original-recipe pastries and homemade mozzarella reminiscent of Arthur Avenue in the Bronx. For those wanting to 'eat in', there's a mini-bar and dining room.

A wood-fired oven cranks out puffy, slightly charred pizzas with not-quite-so-traditional toppings. Their semolina Italian bread is crafted at their nearby bakery, and the resulting subs border on perfect. A favorite? The Rocky Marciano: spicy sopresatta, sharp provolone, roasted red peppers and olive oil.

Take home some of the best sfogliatelle you may ever put into your mouth, along with pignoli/almond cookies, ricotta cookies, eclairs and Italian wedding cookies. If you're lucky, they'll have the lemon ones. If you're really lucky, you might even get a seat in the dining area.

WES ART SCE
AN ENCLAVE OF ARTISTS

riving art scene encompasses a
ge of styles, subjects, and talents.
of nature and the sea, the partic-
he local light infused with ocean
atively inexpensive cost of living
centers has made the area an en-
within the mid-Atlantic region.
resident artists are possessed of
onal resumes, some are impas-
s.

a rich one. For informed collec-
galleries and options to tour artist
earby Rehoboth Art League is an
ation, with a permanent museum
xhibitions and sales.

Art Show, an annual event since
o the streets of downtown Lewes,
first week of July. It is a showing
and energy, combining a broad
a. Exhibitors display paintings,
elry, textiles, and more on Sec-
t Streets (along with a silent auc-
heon). It has grown to now
cal and nationally recognized

artists and artisans. The event is
St. Peter's Episcopal Church Wor
funds for local charities.

Another great event is the A
Artists' Studio Tour. Now in it's
open studio tour is a festive and in
tunity to visit the studio spaces
dozen local painters, sculptors, po
mosaic and stained glass artisan
website at www.lewesart.com.

The Rehoboth Art League, fou
on spacious grounds that date fro
grant, offers year-round classes in
tery, printmaking and sculpture.
includes exhibition opportunitie
sional training nestled in an idy
setting that abuts the Canal. Here
rub shoulders with the eager ama
the bar for all and creating an info
creative community. ■

By Stephanie Bell
Stephanie Bell is an artist and ar

MAGICAL REALISM OF SKY AND SEA

Connoisseurs with a savvy eye for coastal art are quick to point out 'an Abraxas sky or seascape'. Such instant recognition is apt testimony to the distinctive style of Abraxas Hudson, perhaps Lewes' best-known painter. Befitting such recognition and popularity, he has his own highly successful gallery, studio (and adventure gear store!) at 123 Second Street.

Growing up along the Delaware coastline, Abraxas has been working and honing his skills since he was 14, a traditional realist enthralled with color looking for the link connecting the masters from whom he learned and the inspiration of the ever-changing natural beauty that surrounds him.

Amplification of light and attention to detail are the hallmarks of my work, my goal is to make ordinary scenes ex-traordinary. Spectacular places need fewer enhancements and I enjoy painting them, but I really like it when people pause to appreciate the subtle beauty of nature and the world around them.

If my work helps to bring attention to that which is overlooked or taken for granted, I've done my job. We can all benefit from increased awareness.

The most challenging aspect of painting in my style of illuminated realism is choosing which areas of the painting to amplify with light and color and which to subdue.

Choice can be a challenge. Having limitless options but committing to one particular direction for a painting takes confidence. When painting on location, the direction and color of light is ever changing, which can dramatically affect the visual qualities of a scene.

These changes, whether subtle or pronounced, offer the artist many possibilities. Fortunately, painters aren't limited to what they perceive so I keep a compass in my painting bag to ensure that the direction of sunlight I choose in my painting is possible.

Once I find my subject I'll spend several hours on sight refining and laying down in color, light and composition the intricate transitions that occur throughout the day.

I never use black, white or grey and I try to push my color to the edge, a practice requiring a delicate balance between nature and expressionism. Each painting can take months to complete.

My favorite artists are the Hudson River School painters. Their ability to glorify nature is something I strive to do. Some say the fact that they were painting 150 years ago makes their style outdated or not as relevant as some more modern movements. But I say the opposite is true.

Whether we immerse ourselves in actual landscapes or find calm in a well-executed image of a beautiful place, the observation of natural beauty can be quite therapeutic. I hope my paintings inspire people to get outside.

I don't know if there's such a thing as 'Lewes light'. Every place on earth shares the same sun, so it's the minute atmospheric variations that determine an area's quality of light. Particles in the atmosphere, whether man made or natural, affect the penetration of solar rays and result in the cool blue of day or warm light that brackets the day.

Our area is known for beautiful sunsets and that may be true but since I'm in the business of studying them around the world, I say no matter where we are if we can take a moment and appreciate the fleeting beauty of sunrise or sunset, we are doing ourselves a favor. ∎

LEWES _Art Scene_

BARBARA WARDEN

Barbara Warden has created a compelling body of new work in painting/drawing. She views her work as 'studies' where she first explores texture, then line, then scale. In the 'Rockwall' series she builds multiple layers to capture the surface textures of rocks and organisms like lichens.

bfwarden@juno.com
302-645-2735

PAT STABY/ MARKET STREET STUDIOS

Pat Staby, a fiber artist, creates whimsical pillows and wall hangings. Her colorful creations are at one and the same time witty, delightful and decorative pieces.

candletwo@comcast.net
302-645-9030

STEVE ROGERS/ MARKET STREET STUDIOS

Steve Rogers paints marine and landscape scenes in acrylics of the Delmarva Peninsula and the coast of Maine.

candletwo@comcast.net
302-645-9030

LORELEI MEANOR

Lorelei, a mosaic artist, uses the Henlopen region's abundant nature for inspiration along with found objects that she often includes in her artwork. She loves the use of different textures and colors that make her mosaics pop.

www.OceansideMosaics.com
lmeanor@comcast.net
302-703-2660

KEVIN FLEMING

Kevin has covered the world as a photographer for National Geographic. Photographs from his two newest books, 'Wild Delaware' and 'Wild Delmarva' are exhibited in his studio.

www.KevinFleming.com
kfleming@dmv.com
302-542-2922

AINA NERGAARD-NAMACK

Aina had a solo exhibit at Rehoboth's Philip Morton Gallery in 2012 and has had her work exhibited in numerous national juried shows. Her focus is on non-objective paintings inspired by buildings and nature.

www.Nergaard-Nammack.com
ainanerg@verizon.net
302-645-5473

LEWES Art Scene

CONNIE BALLATO

Connie 'paints' with glass creating beautiful stained glass windows and fused glass art for homes, gardens, business and churches. She is an expert in restoration and repair.

www.SunGlassStudio.net
302-645-9431

CONSTANCE COSTIGAN

Constance's images emerge from layers of graphite ranging from very soft to very hard leads. They are elusive, pensive, meditative observations on time and space, spiritual landscape infused with a luminous effect that passes through layers and reflects back. The subject of a one-woman show and catalogue at the Phillips Collection in Washington, her pieces are in the permanent collections of the Hirshhorn Museum and the George Washington University.

BERT LONG

Working in his attic studio, Bert hand carves whimsical fish, caricatures, Santas and more from eastern white pine, basswood and tupelo.

305 Ocean View Boulevard,
Lewes, DE
carvenwood@comcast.net
302-644-0710

VICTOR LETONOFF

Victor paints portraits, still life and figurative works primarily in oil and watercolor. He is trained and works in a traditional, classic style.

510 Railroad Avenue, Lewes, DE
letonoff@aol.com
302-645-6614

BARBARA PETTERSEN

Barbara's acrylic paintings are panoramas of the Lewes and Rehoboth Beach area. She uses bright color and rich texture and emphasizes strong composition.

www.Barbs-Art.com
barbs-art-studio@comcast.net
302-646-6869

CARYL EKIRCH WILLIAMS

Caryl's illustrated children's book, The Words is available on Amazon/Kindle. In addition, Caryl paints, draws, and does graphic design.

cekirchw@comcast.net
Facebook@TheWrds-
CarylMorgan Williams

LEWES ART GALLERIES

ABRAXAS GALLERY In a unique space created by native son, Abraxas Hudson displays paintings that combine a sensitive appreciation of nature, light and love of the sea with a refined, classical painting technique.
123c Second Street | (302) 645-9119 | AbraxasArt.com

CAPE ARTISTS GALLERY is home to a cooperative space in downtown Lewes where members show their original work and share in the management of this unique shop. Here you'll find an eclectic variety of styles, subjects and unique artistic vision. Members organize workshops to continue their art education and enjoy weekly painting sessions which engage lively critical discussion.
110 Third Street | (302) 644-7733 | capeartists.org

PENINSULA GALLERY A local presence for well over a decade but under new, ambitious ownership for the past several years, Peninsula Gallery displays fine art in one of the largest spaces in Delaware. The goal here is to up-scale the offerings of some 30 painters beyond traditional picturesque seascapes and beach scenes and foster a collection of varied styles featuring local and regional painters.
520 E. Savannah Road | (302) 645-0551 | peninsula-gallery.com

MARKET STREET STUDIOS is owned by painter Steve Rogers and fiber artist Pat Staby. The gallery features the whimsical one-of-a-kind pillows and wall hangings of Staby that are in prestigious permanent collections as well as powerful seascapes by Rogers. The revolving work of other local artists is also on exhibit. Housed in their home, the walk-in visitor is treated to a warm welcome and bird's eye view of 'artists at work.'
328 Market Street | 302-645-9030 | candletwo@comcast.net

BIBLION USED BOOKS AND RARE FINDS Biblion offers a rotating exhibitions of the work of local artists amidst its collection of contemporary and antique books.
205 Second Street | (302) 644-2210 | www.biblionbooks.com

SUN GLASS STUDIO open by appointment, is owned by stain glass designer Connie Ballato. She is also skilled in restoration and repair. Her studio displays a broad collection of decorative glass panels, wall pieces, bird feeders and sculptural objects.
125 Franklin Street | (302) 645-9431 | www.sunglassstudio.net

EWES SHOPPIN

UNIQUE, REASONABLE
AND PLEASURABLE

Shopping in Lewes has taken on a higher level of sophistication as the revitalization of downtown continues to gather momentum. Once strictly utilitarian, the town's shops now feature fashion and style far beyond what first-time visitors expect. But the past hasn't been abandoned to trendiness. There are antiques and collectibles to peruse. As well as specialty shops selling yarn and puzzles. A book-store. And, as befits a beach town, homemade ice cream.

SOMETHING NICE: WOMEN'S APPAREL

AQUAMARINE
114 Second Street
302-644-4550

A curated collection of upscale clothing and accessories. Owner Maureen Eschbach takes care to give the store a touch of whimsy and the clothing a one-off advantage for discriminating shoppers.

BEACH JETTY
123 Second Street
302-645-4606 and
205 Market Street
302-644-4608

With two locations downtown, both stores offer women's clothing with a flair and elegance that works equally well dressed up or down. Beach Jetty's reputation for classy casual design has put it on the map amongst fashion cognoscenti.

BLOOMING BOUTIQUE
118 Second Street
302-644-4052

Casual and dress-wear, hats, jewelry are offered at affordable prices. Accessory items are another reason to drop in, like Troll Beads which have developed a loyal following.

THE COTTAGE
142 Second Street
302-644-1544

A gift boutique that offers 'a trip back in time' with authentic vintage ware, an assortment of one-of-a-kind items, clothing, jewelry and accessories, chosen by owner Sally Lawton with her deft eye that combines a feminine touch with a Victorian feel.

CORAL COVE
130 Second Street
302-645-1612

Coral Cove features small household accessories, jewelry and clothing in colors and textures. Handmade jewelry and coin charms lend an 'island flavor' to this high-end hideaway.

COTTON COMPANY
103 Second Street
302-644-2321

Expect to find sophisticated resort wear in this classy little clothing store. Don't let the name fool you, this is no silk-screen t-shirt shop.

DEANNA'S
113 Second Street
302-644-1112

One-half of a combined store space with Piccolino, this boutique offers upscale ladies clothing, gifts, accessories and shoes.

PICCOLINO
111 Second Street
302-644-7611

Find high-end fashions at this longtime Lewes clothing store which joined with Deannas to share a combined store space and offer more stylish ladies outerwear and accessories.

TWILA FARRELL
122 Second Street
302-645-7007

Twila Farrell offers women's apparel from casual to dressed-up on an open sales floor with a large shoe section to the rear. Look for hats, handbags and sleepwear along with easy-care fashions in natural fibers.

VERY EUROPEAN BOUTIQUE
125 Second Street
302-644-7778

An eclectic collection of jewelry, clothing home décor and lingerie, this boutique pushes the limits – while classical music plays in the background.

MARSHA'S
112 Front Street
302-644-4400

A t-shirt shop unlike any other, Marsha "doesn't do frumpy." Instead, she designs and produces apparel that's more like casual fashion. Recylables are big here, and beautiful ear rings hand-made by Costa Rican women.

MORE THAN TRINKETS: GIFTS

FLOWERS BY MAYUMI
128 Second Street
877-644-4468

Although a great deal of Mayumi's flower arranging business is the result of weddings, baby births and other major life events, she maintains a downtown storefront for 'drop-in' impulse buys.

LEWES GIFTS
118 Second Street
302-644-7880

Lewes Gifts offers a variety of all those things that are always nice to have like candles, lotions, lamps, stationary and souvenirs. This is also the place to find logo merchandise like shirts, mugs, and plates as tokens from the beach.

TWO FRIENDS
205 Second Street (across Market Street from Half Full)
302-644-0477

Two Friends offers home décor and house decorations that convey a mood of relaxed style and whimsy. The stars of the show are the large selection of Vera Bradley quilted bags, beach-perfect jewelry and wall hangings with an attitude ("When Nothing Goes Right, Go Left").

THE STEPPING STONE
107 W. Market Street
302-645-1254

More like a gallery than a shop, displaying American handicraft 'curated' by owner Sandy Phalean. The collection includes low-fire pottery dishes and serving plates, ceramics, pendant lights, and a vast display of dangling glass balls.

BIBLION USED BOOKS
205 Second Street
302-644-2210

This independent bookstore is the place to keep your library circulating, as many frequent buyers sell their gently used books on consignment for new reads. Proprietor Jen Mason is always willing to help track down a first edition.

OBJECTS OF DESIRE: JEWELRY, ANTIQUES AND BEAUTIFUL THINGS

JEWELRY EXCHANGE OF DELAWARE
142 Second Street
302-644-3435

Everything here was "previously loved," vintage pieces (and contemporary too) from estates and consignment. An ever-changing collections of antique filigrees, hand-carved cameos, Italian diamonds, precious gemstones, and luxury watches.

ANTIQUE CORNER
401 Kings Highway
302-645-2400

Just off the beaten path, Antique Corner occupies part of an old Victorian home housing a treasure of small furnishings, cutlery, and pottery.

CHATELAINE'S ANTIQUE JEWELRY
119 Second Street
302-645-1511

Offering antique jewelry diamond engagement rings, persian rugs and furnishings, Chatelaine's specializes in fine merchandise. Diamond engagement rings make up a large part of the business, but don't overlook the French greeting cards or line of purses

HABERSHAM PEDDLER
139 Second Street
302-645-8383

Selected Delaware's best 'downstate' furniture store, Habersham Peddler specializes in Colonial American furnishings, many the work of Delaware craftsmen, such as a William and Mary-style maple highboy (a year in the making).

LEWES MERCANTILE ANTIQUES
109 Second Street
302-645-7900

Collectible, vintage, reproduction and antique items acquired from as many as 30 dealers. Eclectic and time-honored, the antique furniture, lighting, pottery, art and lawn accessories make for original accents.

PRESERVATION FORGE
114 W. Third Street
302-645-7987

Artist John Ellsworth, the last local working blacksmith, produces wonderful items for home and garden. Also available for commissioned pieces.

TREASURES
116 Second Street
302-644-1660

With sterling silver jewelry and shiny things for the home, Treasures carries brand-name jewelry and Lori Bonn charms. Fine ornaments here can make Christmas in July a reality.

SAND N STONES
112 Front Street
302-645-0576

Michele Buckler's shop is dedicated to Delaware Nature in assorted forms. Its well known for sea glass (she is an ardent collector) but there's also photographs, books, and stones. She hand-makes the wire-wrap jewelry.

FUN AND GAMES

GINGER MOON FINE YARNS AND ANTIQUES
107 W. Market St.
302-644-2970

Owner Evie McPhee offers uncommon designer yarns outside the mainstream. Like chunky-thick merino wool blended with ostrich feathers, or hand painted, textured yarns. Knitting enthusiasts travel from afar to this shop.

PUZZLES
108 Front Street
302-645-8013

A shop entirely devoted to the pursuit of solving intellectual challenges be they cross-word, jig-saw, or manipulative brain teaser. A tie for the toughest between 32,000 piece puzzle vs. cross-word collection of only vowel-less words.

LEWES GOURMET
110 Front Street
302-645-1661

"Hard to find food items" that span a gamut from locally made jellies to chutneys and curries. For bakers, there's flavorings from A (almond, amaretto) to V (seven kinds of vanilla) with

SWEET THINGS: CANDY, CHILDREN AND PETS

EDIE BEES
115 Second Street
302-645-2337

Edie Bees Confection Shop could make even Willy Wonka grow weak in the knees with 220 apothecary jars of hard candies arranged by color and high-end chocolates.

P.U.P.S. (Pawsitively Unique Pet Shop)
117 Second St.
302-645-9010

P.U.P.S. sells merchandise for positively unique furry friends, everything from shampoos and dog beds to all-natural treats.

KIDS KETCH
132 Second Street
302-645-8448

Toy trucks, toy trains, puzzles, baby dolls, finger puppets, tea sets, coloring books and board games for the young and not-so-young.

A SPORTING TIME: GEAR AND MENS' OUTFITTERS

EAST OF MAUI
34 Cape Henlopen Drive
302-827-4466

This technicolor, two-story East of Maui surf shop en route to Cape Henlopen, bicycles, skateboards and paddleboards available for rent or purchase.

SHOREBREAK
115 Savannah Road
302-645-8488

Has easy-going men's outfitter offering casual, classic menswear that embodies the laid-back vibe of coastal Delaware.

TIDERUNNERS' BAIT & TACKLE
105 Anglers Road
302-645-8866

Gear up before a fishing expedition or get that all-important fishing license. Be sure to stop back and post a picture of your catch for their 'Braggin' Board'.

LEWES CYCLE SPORTS
526 East.Savannah Road
Beacon Motel
888-800-2453

Offering professional repairs for bicycles along with rentals and sales, Lewes Cycle Sports has everything to keep riders cruising from beach cruisers to mountain and road bikes.

QUEST PADDLESPORTS RENTALS
514 East Savannah Road
302-745-2925

With single and tandem kayaks available for rentals as well as guided and private tours (dolphin, full moon and sunset tours are the favorites), Quest makes adventures in paddling easy.

Lewes Diversions
Entertainment

The pleasures of Lewes extend far afield in a variety of directions.

As a seacoast town, there's ocean fishing and boating. And kayaking and canoeing that can take a paddler on journeys of discovery into the wetlands. The landscape is flat, ideal for short jaunts on a bicycle or longer treks through the rural landscape. Lewes has a respected vineyard on its outskirts, making wines that win international awards.

For days when the kids need to be amused, there are short road-trips to nearby farms and nature centers. And don't forget the ghost tour!

A TOWN STEEPED IN FISHING

While the days of commercial fishing have come and gone, sports and leisure fishing are not only alive and well---but in some cases actually getting better.

Vacationers and day-trippers have multiple public access areas and fishing piers at their disposal. Public boat launching ramps, charter and head boat fishing are also available.

Before you begin fishing you must obtain a Delaware fishing license. If you are not a resident, visitor's licenses are available. Crabbers are also required to have a license, which is available at tackle shops in the area.

The fishing season is year-round in Lewes. There's always something biting. Spring brings with it excellent Stripped Bass, Tautog and Flounder fishing. Summer is prime time with Flounder, Spot, Croaker, Puppy Drum, Sea Trout and Stripped Bass in abundance. Fall is the season to catch monster Stripped Bass and Blue Fish in the surf. Winter is the season to go out on one of the head or charter boats for Sea Bass or Tog.

The Lewes Canal is a Flounder hot spot mid-April thru early October. The spots to go are the City Dock in Canalfront Park or the Roosevelt Inlet at the mouth of the canal. The tides move rapidly thru the canal so ample tackle and weight are required to keep your bait on or near the bottom. Jigs and Gulp(tm) jerk shad will catch flounder as well.

Stripped Bass and Sea Trout can be caught in the canal as well as the fishing pier in Henlopen State Park. Live Minnows, cut Mullet and Spot are great baits for these fish. Early morning and late evening are the best time to go after them.

Spot and Croaker are abundant during the summer months and are fun and very easy to catch. They can be found about anywhere you decide to fish. Night Crawlers and Blood Worms are by far the most effective baits to use for them.

There are many other species that can be caught in the waters around Lewes. Local tackle shops are great places to get the latest info on all fishing in the area and are highly recommended to visit before a great day of fishing!

Lastly, only keep the fish you know you're going to eat and release the rest. Always clean up after yourself to keep the town tidy and the fish happy! ∎

By Howard Hundley
Avid fisherman and environmentalist Howard Hundley writes for various publications and looks forward to a bright future fishing local waters.

ONCE YOU CATCH A FISH, YOU'RE HOOKED AND ALWAYS COME BACK

I migrated here from the west coast, Newport Beach, California where I grew up. Out there, it's more rocky with deep water 500 feet just a mile off-shore. In Delaware, the continental shelf is 70 miles away so there's a lot more room to fish. I like it here because Lewes feels more homey.

The Pirate King II is a charter boat, it's licensed for 100 miles offshore but usually we only go out 23 miles to fish the artificial reefs. Occasionally we'll go out further if we're going after tuna or tilefish because that's where you find them.

We start out the summer fishing season with a three hour trout fishing trip for kids. I've had two and three year olds going out for the first time in their lives, and they'll still be showing up twenty years later. It seems that once they catch a fish, they're hooked and they always come back.

In season, beginning from spring through fall, we run six hour fishing trips. We usually go hunting for fish along the reef sites, these are artificial fish havens that are sunk in the water to attract fish. There are eight numbered sites in the bay and three out in the ocean going down to Rehoboth.

Flounder is our most popular fish because they're the easiest to catch. They feed off the bottom so a simple drop line will catch them most times. Most everybody likes the way flounder tastes, it's bland without the heavy 'fishy' taste. People like to catch trout a lot, too.

Tautog is real popular, then comes sea bass. Rockfish or Stripers used to be real good here through the 1990s but now they seem to be declining in numbers. We used to go out seven days a week fishing for Stripers, even eight years ago you could go out and be assured of catching your limit. Now the boats are just sitting here. It might be the economy, but people don't want to go out unless they're going to catch something.

We run two types of shark trips during the summer. One is for the kids to catch Sand sharks because they don't have any teeth. We have little kids going out and catching their first shark or finfish, it's a big thing for them. The other is for the adults where we go after the pelagic sharks, which have teeth. We catch them in the bay and out in the ocean.

We usually go fishing all the time in the summer when the weather is good but during the fall and spring we stay at the dock when the wind is blowing more than 25 knots. It's too difficult to fish under those conditions on the deck of a boat.

During the summer, in the afternoon we get some thunderstorms rolling through where it can go from flat calm to a 70-mile-an-hour wind in a period of five minutes. This will last from ten minutes to a half hour, and then it calms right out again. These kinds of storms aren't a daily thing but they'll appear once or twice a week depending on temperature and how much humidity is in the air.

It can get exciting coming up the shoot into the bay when there's a northwest wind against a flood tide. I've been on a boat that's been struck by lightening a couple of times, that literally makes your hair stand on end.

When Hurricane Sandy rolled through here in 2012, the fishing went down to nothing because the storm was like a big roto-rooter going across the bottom. It silted everything up and covered the food sources. It took a lot of tidal washes to clean things up, nine months or so until we started catching fish again. ■

BOATING

Lewes has been a nautical town since its beginnings as a whaling outpost. Recreational boating here, however, is of a lesser scale than elsewhere on the Delmarva coast. In the last few years, say local watermen, the combination of the Great Recession and more rigorous fishing regulations have taken a toll on the boating population. Even so, boating enthusiasts find much to love here with the town dock ideally located at the center of a very cruiser-friendly town.

With the establishment of its first Dockmaster in 1935, the Lewes harbor became more formalized. That's a good thing because the waterfront here (as is the case throughout Delaware) is limited. There's extensive marshland, but not equally limitless stretches to dock boats.

The Dockmaster (302-644-1869, dockmaster@ci.lewes.de.us), among other duties, manages the City's boat slip availability. There are public facilities along Front Street on the southern bank of the Canal about one mile in from the Roosevelt Inlet (just past the lightship Overfalls).

Canalfront Park Marina has 19 boat slips, 13 of which are reserved for Lewes residents. Transients can reserve slips as available: two large slips can accommodate boats up to 55 feet in length and 16 foot beam; four small slips can accommodate 25 feet in length and 12 foot beam. The dredged water depth in the Marina is generally six feet (plus or minus) mean low water.

The 200 foot long Otis B. Smith City Dock, located further south along Front Street, is sectioned into four 50 foot slips that can accommodate small and large vessels. Mean low water height is dredged to eight feet.

Fisherman's Wharf (Angler's Road and Savannah Highway, 302-645-8862), on the other side of the Canal, has 26 slips, some of which are available to transients. Most are meant for boats with a 15-16 foot beam and length of 45-70 feet, although boats as long as 110 feet have been accommodated here.

J.B. Walsh at Angler's Marina (217 Angler's Road, 302-645-7981) is a helpful source for boaters who run into mechanical problems. While they don't fix boats at his shop, they can help identify somebody who can (and pull a boat out of the water, if need be). ■

Finding a boat any bigger than a kayak to rent to rent is hard to do in Lewes but in nearby Dewey Beach (8 miles), boats can be rented from Delaware Marine Group (1905 Highway One, 302-227-7796).

THE KALMAR NYCKEL

Throughout much of August, Lewes harbor takes on the ambiance of the grand age of sea-farers when a three-masted, eight square-sailed Tall Ship ties up at the public pier of the Ferry terminal. She is the Kalmar Nyckel, a modern-day replica of the Swedish square-rigger that brought the first permanent European inhabitants to Fort Christina (which would later become Wilmington) on a mid-winter crossing in 1638.

Having begun her life in the 1620s as a Dutch merchant vessel, she was purchased and outfitted as a war ship to defend the Baltic port city of Kalmar by its Swedish citizens and then, several years later, confiscated by the crown and presented to a private trading company to colo-nize what would eventually become Delaware.

Some three hundred years later, a foundation re-created the Kalmar Nyckel as a tribute to those original settlers. She was launched in 1997: 94 feet long, with a 25 foot beam, 12 foot draft, and a two-tailed lion figurehead on the bow.

With its full-time captain and crew, the ship serves as an outreach platform for the State of Delaware and also provides sea-based educational programming. Morning and afternoon sails are open to the public while she is in Lewes (book in advance, 302-429-7477). Private charter sails can be specially arranged by special arrangement. ∎

KAYAKING AND CANOING

Lewes is a prime site for paddling, offering first timers and veterans a full range of opportunities from surf to wetlands. One poetic insider describes what it's like to canoe or kayak here, amidst the "steady flow of the tributaries flowing in the Bay, the murmuring of currents through the marshes as they rise and fall with the steady breathing of the tides."

Visitors can choose between guided tours or solo explorations.

Cape Henlopen State Park offers ocean kayak rental to those who are at least 18 years old (children 8-13 can accompany an adult in a tandem). On lucky days, you'll be able to see dolphins breaching as they cruise the Point. The Park conducts Sunset Kayaking Tours on Tuesday evenings at 6:30, two-hour paddles out to the Breakwater (nesting osprey have been sighted there). They're limited to ten (kids must be 10

years old), so reserve in advance at the Nature Center (302-645-6852).

Private rental companies like Quest Kayak also offer sunset cruises. Matt Carter, a partner in Quest who has been paddling here since 1999, celebrates the personal view of marine life one gets. "When you paddle along the outer and inner wall, the dolphins are so close you can see their eyes staring at you. The beach gets quiet and occasionally you get the aroma of the Lewes Bake Shop roasting coffee. It's beautiful, you're looking at the day going to sleep."

A put-in at Canalfront Park makes it easy to get into the Canal. You can head all the way to Rehoboth, passing under the drawbridge. Getting through the railroad swing bridge can be exciting, nothing scary but you'll need some endurance going against the tide. Drifting beside the grassy banks along the east side of the canal, populated by colonies of tiny little mud crabs, makes for a peaceful meander.

Going north on the Canal in the other direction leads past historic houses along Pilottown Road and the docked ships of the University of Delaware maritime campus, to Canary Creek, a cut into wetlands accessible only by boat. The entry is under a low-beam fishing bridge. Insiders wax enthusiastic about the amazing variety of wildfowl and marine critters to be seen in these waters. (For those who want to save their energy, there's a public boat ramp at the end of Pilottown Road a few hundred yards up-stream from the entry to the marsh).

You can follow the Canal north into the Broadkill, which will then take you all the way to Milton. The paddle to this charming town that was once a boat-building center makes for interesting sights but it is recommended only for experienced paddlers with the stamina to handle the four hour trip and the skill to negotiate the swift current of the tidal cycles. Wind conditions can also add to the challenge.

Old Mill Creek is a stream fed from Red Mill Pond that is a tributary of the Broadkill, joining the river about a mile upstream from its mouth at the Bay. Sharp bends of this snaking creek can pose a challenge to even accomplished paddlers. There's wildlife to be sighted along the way as it borders the Great Marsh Preserve---black ducks, kingfishers, great blue herons, snowy egrets and turtles. One put-in harkens back to pioneer days, on Route 1 about a mile north of Lewes look for an unmarked, unpaved road running east, across from Red Mill Pond. A more conventional way to get in (or do a shuttle) is the boat launch at the end of Oyster Road, which intersects Route One about 1.5 miles north of Red Mill Pond.

Prime Hook National Wildlife Refuge has a seven-mile long water trail, with a launch at the parking lot at the Refuge office and another at Waples Mill Pond (see below). As befits a national refuge, there is an abundance of nature to savor: white cedar, sweet gum, green ash, winterberry bushes, the large pink and white blooms of marsh mallow in August attract butterflies.

Brumley's Family Park, at the intersection of Route 5 and Route 1 (two miles past Route 16, 18 miles from Lewes) offers a private ramp at Waples Mill Pond that insiders recommend as a great way to paddle Prime Hook Creek along the western boundary of the national wildlife refuge. It's also the recommended entry for those planning to do the entire course to the Broadkill. The first portion of the trail winds through a red maple swamp that is spectacular when the leaves change color in the fall. ■

Rentals and guided tours of the Atlantic, the Bay, or the backwater are available from Quest Fitness and Kayak (302-745-2925) and East of Maui Surf Shop (302-827-4466)

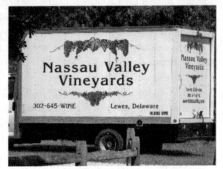

NASSAU VALLEY VINEYARDS

It takes ten minutes to get to the Nassau Valley Vineyards from downtown Lewes, considerably closer than going to Napa Valley. Judging from the vineyard's success in international competitions, their wines can handle the comparison. Visitors can judge for themselves from tastings offered how the local Delmarva 'terroir' stacks up.

Throughout its 20 years of wine-making, Nassau Valley has expanded and refined its grape plantings. Current offerings include varietals Cabernet Sauvignon, Chardonnay, Pinot Grigo as well as blends (Indian River Red is made along the model of a classic French Bordeaux from Cab Franc, Cab Sauvignon, and Merlot). Specialty wines show up as available, made from local blueberries, peaches, and a grape called Delaware White.

Tours are self-guided, through five galleries of exhibits that offer a quick introduction to the eight thousand year history of wine and wine making. Who knew that the Egyptians invented the wine press or that it takes at least fifteen leaves to ripen one cluster of grapes?

Private guided tours are available by appointment for groups of fifteen or more. As are specialty tastings and wine and food pairings (on-site or off) outside of peak season by special arrangement.

Nassau Valley Vineyard is open for touring Monday through Saturday (11 am to 5 pm) and Sunday (noon to 5 pm). Admission with tasting is $10, participants must be 21 years old and can take home their etched crystal tasting glass as a souvenir. ∎

36 Nassau Commons, Lewes, DE 19958
(302) 645-9463

'WE'RE PUTTING DELAWARE ON THE MAP, ONE WINE AT A TIME'

I grew up on our father's farm where we were all forced labor in the hay field so I wanted nothing to do with agriculture.

After college at American University, I got a job in D.C. working for Les Amis du Vin International, the first publication in the U.S. about wine. I received a very charmed wine education, I learned from the best people in the business. After a few years, I got tired of writing about other people's wine and decided to make my own.

My father planted five rows of vines in 1987 to get me back home (my parents still live in the house on Lewes Beach where we grew up).

You were prohibited in Delaware at that time from having a functioning winery that sold directly to the public. The state alcohol laws required all sales to be through licensed retail stores. We finally got the law changed in 1991 and for a dozen years we were the only winery in the state. We launched Nassau Valley Vineyards in 1993.

For a long time, conventional wisdom was that you couldn't grow vinifera, the classic wine grapes, on the Delmarva coast. People would blame the humidity, but they wrongly forgot that our growing conditions here are far more similar to Europe than is California. France is humid. To be sure, humidity presents a challenge that California doesn't have because it's arid climate means growers don't have to worry about mildew.

Grapes take well here. The maritime climate and the presence of the Atlantic resemble Bordeaux in France. The land is well suited to growing vines that like chalky, rocky soil for drainage. It helps that we're sitting on twenty feet of sand. That keeps the roots healthy.

We have such a long growing season that there's no trouble ripening Cabernet Sauvignon. Our August would brutalize Pinot Noir, and Riesling needs a colder climate, but we've got a wide variety of other vinifera like Cabernet Franc, Merlot, and Chardonnay in the vineyard that do well.

2010 was a great vintage. It was hot and dry. You sacrifice some yield in that kind of a year but you make up for it in the quality of the fruit. When there's lots of rain, the vines suck up the water and this dilutes the fruit. We still have some 2010 for sale. 2006 was another great year but a small vineyard like us that produces five thousand cases a year can't afford to keep inventory to age. That's up to the customer.

There are characteristic fruit notes to our wines. Lemon and pear with Chardonnays, a lot of black cherry with the reds. Raspberry seems to be predominant with Merlot. These notes come from what wine people call 'terroir', everything that makes a tiny corner of the world special: the air flow over your site, the amount of sun, the fact that the wind can turn around and you get an ocean breeze, the elements in the soil. I call it the 'smagic' (magic with an 's', it's fun to say).

Our main focus in terms of style is to make wines that always remain 'food friendly', wines that aren't so big and obtuse with flavor that it hits you over the head and ruins your palate for anything else. Many domestic chardonnays are an example of what we don't do, Americans have gotten into the habit of barrel fermenting so that all you get is a big mouthful of oak instead of the nuances of the wine.

I like to say 'we're putting Delaware on the map one wine at a time.' We've taken over 150 medals in international competitions; we've been on the stage with wines from all over the world. Even so, you still have to get over the would-be connoisseurs and snobs who are prejudiced by their arrogance against making wine in Delaware. Well-qualified, important wine writers love us. We've earned their kudos. But you get people, locals as well as visitors, who automatically presume that there's no way our wine could be good just because we're here in Lewes.

A favorite quote of mine to puncture wine snobs comes from one of my mentors and an all-time great of wine, Robert Gourdin, who says "the best wines in the world are nothing more than good local wines at home." ∎

PRIME HOOK NATIONAL WILDLIFE REFUGE

Entry to Prime Hook starts at Turkle Pond Road off Route 16 East, about fifteen minutes from Lewes north on Highway One.

Prime Hook National Wildlife Refuge, established in 1963, is part of the national system managed by the US Fish and Wildlife Service that is regarded as the most comprehensive in the world. It was named Priume Hoek (Plum Point) by the Dutch because of the abundance of wild beach plums growing amongst the dunes.

Its ten thousand acres of freshwater and salt marshes, woodlands, grasslands, scrub-brush habitats, ponds, bottomland forested areas, a 7-mile long creek, and agricultural lands provide habitat for approximately 296 species of birds, 38 species of reptiles and amphibians and 37 different mammals. Among the animals residing here are beaver, white-tailed deer, gray and red fox, mink, muskrat, river otter, long-tailed weasel and woodchuck.

Throughout the year a number of programs and tours are conducted for the public at Prime Hook including nature hikes, pond side adventures, and the 'Evening at the Hook Lecture Series'.

As a wildlife refuge whose priority is to preserve a natural habitat rather than provide a visitor-friendly experience, the layout can sometimes be confusing. There are a half-dozen walking trails that are, for the most part, looped to Turkle Pond Road (which, says legend, is so named because the original owner mispronounced 'turtle'). It is wise for first-timers to start at the administration building on the Turkle Road access road for general information and trail maps.

Black Farm Trail, named after the farm that

was previously here, is a 1.6 mile walk through what one insider calls "an enchanted tunnel" of overhanging foliage that feels timeless. Former pastures have been taken over by wildflowers. There is a wooden observation structure along the way, an ideal venue for bird watching or just idle daydreaming.

Pine Grove Trail is .8 miles long, a loop that can be done in 15 minutes which is perfect for small children. Along the way, there is a stunning view of Fleetwood Pond from benches on the walkway dock and a meander beneath tall pines that have been called "the grove's vaulted cathedral."

Blue Goose Tail is the newest and one of the longer in Prime Hook. Its 1.6 miles wanders through an excellent songbird refuge (Eastern Kingbird, Yellow Warbler, Gray Catbird, Common Yellowthroat) and affords a great view of shallow, fresh water Turkle Pond where it is overlooked by a bald eagle nest (the nest is hard to spot). The dense undergrowth at the end of the trail makes it another world, "dark and mysterious."

Birders will find Prime Hook a treasure. It is located on the Atlantic flyway with a sufficiently varied habitat to sustain both migrating shore-birds in the spring and fall as well as nesting wading birds. Ornithologists consider it one of the mid-Atlantic's finest birding spots although it's something of a well-kept secret, overshadowed by the better known Bombay Hook in Kent County.

Hunting and fishing in accordance with state and federal regulations is allowed in Prime Hook. ∎

11978 Turkle Pond Road, Milton, DE 19968
302-684-8419
For maps and details,
www.fws.gov/northeast/primehook/
opportunities

MILTON

Milton is another of Delaware's 'hidden' treasures, small in size (population under 2,000) but big in character and personality, a rewarding 'road trip' only 11 miles from Lewes.

At the heart of Milton (population 2,576 in the 2010 Census) is a charming historical area. It's perfect for a leisurely stroll, followed by an informal meal. On Wednesday evenings in summer, the town sponsors free concerts at Memorial Park that are always lively family entertainment. On Friday afternoons from 3:30-6:00 is a farmer's market.

Wander around Wagamons Pond past a statue erected to John Milton, the poet of *Paradise Lost* (and inspiration for what was finally chosen in 1807 as the town's name). Like Lewes, Milton has more than its share of colonial and Victorian architecture (198 structures on the Federal Historic Register). Bask in the ambiance of the houses along Chestnut and Federal Streets that once belonged to families with 'olde' English names like Hazzard, Paynter, and Betts.

The head of the Broadkill River in Milton was a center of shipbuilding in the mid-19th century when there were nearby forests of ramrod straight Atlantic cypresses and strong white cypresses. These trees were perfect for building the three and four-masted schooners that dominated the oyster dredging industry of the time. These boats were ideally suited for the complicated, fast-changing winds and currents of the Delaware Bay and were likened to "birds of the sea whose swimming is like flying."

After shipbuilding phased out, Milton became a center for button making. Mother-of-pearl shells were shipped here from the Pacific to be cut and polished into button blanks in shops and garages throughout town, then shipped to northeastern garment centers for decoration and use. The soil in many a backyard garden contains sparkling mother-of-pearl pieces.

Milton was also known as the Christmas holly capital of the country, producing more of the shiny, prickly-leaved, red-berried evergreens than anywhere else in the United States.

The Lydia Black Cannon Museum at 210 Union Street, maintained by the Milton Historical Society, offers an overview of four centuries of local history. ■

DOGFISH HEAD BREWERY TOUR

When Dogfish Head began in June, 1995, it may well have been the smallest commercial brewer in America. "Our very first batch, Shelter Pale Ale, was brewed on a system which essentially was three little kegs with propane burners underneath," recalls founder Sam Calagione.

"The one benefit to brewing on such a small system was the ability to try out a myriad of different recipes. We quickly got bored brewing the same things over and over – that's when we started adding all sorts of weird ingredients and getting kind of crazy with the beers!"

Today Dogfish, which one international beer writer calls "America's most interesting and adventurous small brewery," ships more than 20 styles of Dogfish Head beer across the U.S. and into other countries. The Steampunk Treehouse on exhibit is from the famous Burning Man festival (vintage 2007) in Nevada

Visitors to the Milton facility are taken deep into the brewing process. Many call this informative approach their best brewery tour ever. Craft enthusiasts are especially likely to enjoy the Dogfish approach on life in general and beer-making in particular. ∎

Reservations usually required but, even if the tours are booked, sampling is available.
Tuesday-Saturday, 11-5
6 Cannery Village Boulevard, Milton, DE
302-684-1000

ABBOTT'S MILL

Abbott's Mill, thirty minutes north of Lewes, is one of the last water-powered grist mills in Delaware. It is listed on the National Register of Historic Sites, and set amidst a beautiful nature preserve with hiking trails and boardwalks through forested, field and wetland habitats.

Such gristmills used to be virtually everywhere in Delaware. They were the cornerstone of an agricultural economy based on corn and wheat. Abbott's Mill dates back to 1802, when its owner petitioned the Court of General Sessions to extend a new road to reach the mill that he had "at a large expense erected, and just finished." Active until 1960, it is still in working condition and used for educational demonstrations (call in advance to confirm schedule).

The small nature center on the grounds offers Native American displays and wildlife taxidermy. It also maintains a fine collection of live local reptiles, amphibians, and fish. Younger children particularly will find these exhibits interesting. ■

15411 Abbott's Pond Road, Milford, DE 19963 (25 miles from Lewes)
302-422-0847
www.ecodelaware.com

DELAWARE STATE FAIR

The Delaware State Fair, held each summer for about ten days at the end of July, is a wonderful journey into an agricultural life-style largely unknown to most city dwellers. The longer it's been since you've been to a fair, the more you'll enjoy this excellent one's midway, livestock shows, exhibits and food.

The first Delaware Fair was held in 1920, when it was known as the Kent and Sussex County Fair. It remains true to its original mission: "promoting and encouraging Agriculture and giving pleasures and diversions to the inhabitants of rural communities." Annual attendance is around three hundred thousand.

The Fair showcases the talents of youth and their elders in a wide range of livestock, domestic arts, and culinary competitions. Recently a Battle of Home Brews has been added to the schedule, which also features concerts, harness racing, rodeos, tractor pulls, and even a demolition derby.

Among the things a visitor can see on display in vast barns are prize winning cattle, goats, rabbits, chickens, sheep, swine, horses, ponies, and even a category of 'pretty animals'. Few 'city slickers' have any idea how many different, interesting varieties of these species exist and are being raised on Delaware farms. There's also a petting zoo, where young and old have been able to do such things in the past as feed carrots to a giraffe

The domestic arts winners on exhibit in the Dover Building include Needlework, Arts & Crafts, needlework, flower arranging, hat making, and 'star quality' best-in-show fruit, vegetables, and flowers. The results of the different bake-offs are there to be seen (if not sampled) including winners of the contests for 'blueberry blowout,' 'chocolate temptation,' 'peach desert,' and 'wild game'.

Along with over 30 rides on the midway are carnival prizes to be won---including goldfish. When it comes to food, the Fair caters more to guilty pleasures of excess than moderation. Among featured delicacies, along with standard fair fare like corn dogs and funnel cakes, have been deep-fried Oreos, Doughnut Burgers (half-pound meat patty with bacon and cheese served between glazed doughnuts), and Fudge Puppies (a Belgian waffle on a stick served with chocolate fudge). Insiders know to save their appetite for the tasty delicacies offered up by the Mennonite ladies at their food tent. ∎

State Fair Grounds
Harrington, Delaware (30 miles from Lewes)
www.delawarestatefair.com/

CONVERSATION: ERIC KAFKA
Founding Member, Rehoboth Beach Film Society

WE WANTED TO WATCH A DIFFERENT KIND OF FILM

Eric Kafka, a psychologist by profession, is a long-time resident of Lewes.

Sixteen years ago a local group of people said they wanted to watch a different kind of film than the 'Hollywood type of film' shown in theaters. That was the origins of the Rehoboth Beach Film Society. So we set about getting and screening much more plot-driven, character-driven, independent films without major stars and from different countries, as well as documentaries that have grown tremendously here in America in the last 15-20 years.

We did this to avoid having to go to major cities, Baltimore, Washington, or New York City to see these types of films.

The Society is now a formal non-profit membership group with 1500 members, over half of whom are from the Lewes/Rehoboth area. Every month, we show four or five films in local libraries, churches, and schools. We'll have special documentaries about art and the lives of artist's that we screen at the Inn at Canal Square in Lewes. We'll also show films about local history like the 'Storm of '62' or shipbuilding in Milford. During the summer, there are evening films for the family at the Canalfront Park in Lewes as well as the Pavilion in Rehoboth and we have a day camp for children where they can make their own film.

We're best known for our annual film festival that takes place over 5 days at the Midway Theaters on Route One. It's grown into a relatively big deal, drawing people from almost two-dozen states. It's usually the second weekend in November, Wednesday through Sunday.

We select 110 documentary and feature films, there's also seminars given by screenwriters and directors talking about various aspects of filmmaking.

Each year we highlight the films of a particular country with about eight films from that country included with talks and special live performances. One year we featured Italy, the year before that it was India.

There is no glamour or red carpet treatment here. We charge very reasonable ticket prices. There's food and drinks available from local restaurants in a big tent area right behind the movie house so there's constant circulation of people coming in and out of the films with a place to sit down and eat and talk. You'll find a certain kind of artistic sense and intellect that you have in common with the other people here, you can strike up a very good friendship at your table under the tent with your dinner and your drink or waiting in line with them for the next film.

People can get their tickets in advance or on the day of the screening (although a word to the wise: more than a few sell out). ∎

LEWES HISTORICAL SOCIETY TOURS

The Lewes Historical Society offers a number of tours designed to bring the town's past alive in the present. Topics range from cemeteries to lighthouses. There's even one about haunted houses.

Tickets are $10 for adults (children free except when noted) and can be purchased at the Ryves Holt House Museum Gift Shop (218 Second Street). Call ahead for times and schedules (302-645-76710).

MUSEUM TOUR:

This tour features a guided walk-about on the grounds of Historical Society Complex, at Shipcarpenter Street and West Third Street. There are nine historic buildings, dating from the early 1700s, all but one moved from other Sussex County sites. They include a doctor's office, blacksmith shop, one-room school house and several houses that were quite grand in their time. A must for history buffs.

MARITIME TOUR

Lewes has been shaped from its earliest day by its relationship to the water, looking outward to the Atlantic and inward to the Bay. This guided walking tour focuses on ships and sailors with a narrative that begins with the first explorers from Europe. The stroll wends down Second Street to the Life-Saving Station, along the Canal and ends with a visit to the collection of maritime artifacts in the Cannonball House.

ARCHITECTURAL TOUR

With its vintage houses from different ages, Lewes is a veritable museum of America's architectural past. This tour through the historical district presents a sampling of that collection, ranging from one of the oldest house in the state to stately Victorians.

HISTORIC LEWES TROLLEY TOUR

The one hour, five-and-a-half mile circuit affords a fun, air-conditioned way to get a broad perspective of town. A little bit of everything is offered including history, architecture, and tales about the people who have lived here.

MARITIME TROLLEY TOUR

Another trolley tour, this one water-centric. The focus is on Lewes history from the perspective of the sea, with the route through Cape Henlopen State Park. Visitors will learn about lighthouses, breakwaters, quarantine station, Fort Miles and the defense of the Bay in times of war.

HAUNTED HOUSE TOUR

If you believe in ghosts---or, at least are willing to suspend judgment---this is a tour for you. History is traced through the events and people that have left their imprint (and perhaps their spirits) here, from pirates to veterans of the War of 1812. This tour will highlight some of the grand old characters who lived here and the paranormal phenomena they may have left behind.

SELF-GUIDED MARITIME TOUR

Throughout Lewes is 4.3 mile trail with signage pointing out maritime attractions for those who prefer self-guided tours (brochures and maps available at the Visitors Center and Historical Society). It begins at the University of Delaware Marine Sciences campus, past the 1812 Park and the Cannonball House, a viewing of the lighthouses from Lewes Beach, and ending at the fishing pier at Cape Henlopen State Park.

GHOST TOUR
The Hauntings of Hoorkill

I met Russ Allen, president of the Lewes Historical Society, at the Ryves Holt House gift shop one chilly afternoon for a 'private showing' of the ghost tour he gives in October. He advised me to download a "Ghost Radar" application to track electromagnetic field changes for some added theatrics but there was insufficient space on my smartphone.

As we began, I ask him where the ghosts hang out in this old town.

"Well, we date back to 1631," he said. "The whole colony was massacred. Where do we start?"

First stop was the Ryves Holt House, one of the oldest homes in the nation, surely a good place to find spirits lurking. The Ghost Radar app usually shows activity centered at the stairways, which happens to be where a psychic once told Allen she saw a teenager with consumption being pushed. Records do, indeed, confirm that a woman died falling down the stairs of this old house.

Our next stop was St. Peter's graveyard and the final resting place of Captain James Drew, of H.M.S. *DeBraak*, a ship that sank in Lewes harbor in 1798 killing Drew and most of his crew. The legend of the Bad Weather Witch was borne of this tragedy. Sailing under the British flag, the ship had recently captured a Spanish galleon. Coming into Lewes port after months of harsh ocean travel, the sloop-of-war ignored ship pilots' advice about heavy weather and took anchor off-shore. She was turned on her side by a strong gust of wind and filled with water immediately. Still carrying Spanish P.O.W.s and an estimated $500 million in gold, the ship sank in minutes. Three Spanish prisoners later came ashore with the captain's trunk and pockets full of gold coins (they were the source for folklore about riches that went down with the ship).

Captain Drew's body washed ashore days later and he was buried in St. Peter's Meanwhile,

33 members of his crew were buried at another site near the Zwaanendael Museum. Ever since, Drew's ghost is said to have been seen, searching the graveyard for his crew.

The Bad Weather Witch is thought to be responsible for taking down the gold-laden ship for its purse. She guarded the treasure through the centuries, causing storms whenever hunters came looking for it. One captain even sought to exorcise the witch in 1935 by burning her symbolically at the stake, an effort that only brought more storms. In 1986, modern technology won a small battle against superstition when the hull of the *DeBraak* was raised but even then the Bad Weather Witch got the last laugh. Little gold or treasure was recovered in the excavation.

From the graveyard, we headed toward Third Street where Allen recalled a tale about a house owned by John and Hetty Metcalf in the late 1800s.

Despite that expression of spiritual completion etched on her tombstone ("I have fought a good fight, I have finished my course"), there are reports that Hetty still haunts her former home. She misses her cat, so it is said. And she grows lonely when the house's residents are absent. One incident stands out as particularly eerie. The current owner of the house purchased a new quilt and, before leaving for the week, put it atop the bed she made. Upon her return, she found the bed stripped. The new quilt lay crumpled in the corner. Her explanation: Hetty must not have liked her taste!

On to the Cannonball House on Front Street, which Allen calls the most haunted house in Lewes.

In 1917, the house was a notions store owned by 88-year-old Susan King Rowland, who kept an apartment in the back. Two days after World War I was declared, she closed up shop and went to prepare dinner in the fireplace of her quarters.

She would not live to see the resolution of the War. That night, Susan's dress caught fire and she burned to death.

The property was in very bad shape by the time the Historical Society acquired it in 1963. Local craftsman Freddy Hudson agreed to help restore the building and set up shop in the living quarters. After each day of work, he would put his tools on a bench, close the attic door, and lock up the house. Day after day he would return to find his tools on the floor and the attic door open.

He was convinced someone was breaking in at night so he threaded a string through the doorways and windows to have evidence of the intruder's entryway. When he returned the next morning, the tools were again on the floor and the attic door was open. But none of the strings were broken. He became convinced a ghost haunted the building.

Someone suggested to Freddy that if he politely asked the ghost to keep his affairs as he left them, she might oblige. He tried that approach. One evening before closing up, he explained to Susan, "I know you don't like my tools on the bench, but I really need to keep them off the floor. And please keep the doors closed. It is very drafty in here and we are trying to keep it warm, so I would appreciate it." Sure enough, from then on the tools weren't moved and the attic door stayed closed.

But Susan remained restless.

After the Cannonball House became a museum, docents reported the door once again began to open at night. One evening, a nail was actually hammered through the door to keep it shut. The next morning, the door was open and the nail was on the floor. Exasperated, the docents resigned themselves to living with this 'mystery'.

That truce, however, didn't last long. The door opens to a narrow, steep stairwell that leads to an old, empty attic. Over-curious museum visitors would trek upstairs despite the perilous climb. Something had to be done to close off access, so the docents decided to screw the door shut with 14 screws and then hide it behind a poster.

Apparently, Susan would have none of this. The next morning, all 14 screws had been removed and the poster was rolled up at the foot of the door. Holes from both botched attempts at permanently closing the door can still be seen. Russ Allen told me this is a spot where the Ghost Radar app goes off-the-charts.

Another Cannonball House tale is spooky. A heavy, ornate treasure chest dating back hundreds of years long rested in the corner of Susan's living chambers. This chest has one key to control dozens of latches on the cover. During the most recent renovation, this room was to be repainted. The painter closed the lid of the chest and worked around it.

The next day, a maintenance man found the treasure chest locked. The groundskeeper searched high and low for the key but couldn't find it. The painter said he had never even seen one!

Locksmiths examined the chest, but stated there was nothing they could do with modern-day equipment As the date approached for the museum to re-open, the decision was made to display the treasure chest as it was, firmly locked shut.

But things changed the day before opening. As the room was being tidied up in preparation, a long coil of rope was discovered by the attic door. To the great surprise of all, the chest's 15th century key was resting just under the rope.

Sightseers beware: Susan has a wicked sense of humor! ∎

By Molly MacMillan

SIGHTSEEING CRUISES

Sightseeing cruises make it easy to get on the water for a few hours of cruising to watch dolphins, whales, or a beautiful sunset.

Trips depart from Fisherman's Wharf on the east side of the Canal, 107 Angler's Road.

One important thing to note, scheduled trips require a minimum number of passengers---if that quota isn't filled, the ship doesn't go out. Call in advance for availability (302-645-8862) but be prepared for this possible 'worst case' scenario (it happens infrequently but folks waiting on the dock will be disappointed should their trip be unexpectedly cancelled).

Dolphin Watching Cruises sail daily from mid-June through early September. They depart at 9:30 a.m. (plan to arrive at least thirty minutes prior to departure) and typically last about two hours. Tickets include a free continental breakfast served on board. "Amazing views of the Atlantic," reported one passenger. "We followed a playful pod of dolphins all the way out, they were so close to the boat at times we could see their little faces."

Afternoon cruises depart at 1:30. At three hours, these last longer and visitors may spot a whale as well as dolphins.

Evening cruises sail each night of the week except Sunday, departing at 7:00 p.m. in June and July (6:30 in August). ■

CAPE WATER TAXI

Cape Water Taxi started in 2012 and now has two boats offering transportation along the coast between Lewes and Dewey Beach on the Canal on Friday, Saturday, and Sunday from June through September and October (weather permitting).

In addition to point-to-point transit, Cape Water Taxi also offers eco tours and ninety-minute sunset cruises (Tuesday-Thursday) along the inland waterway.

For reservations, call 302-644-7334. Walk-on passengers are also accommodated as space permits. The Lewes dock is on Anglers Road, just past Fisherman Wharf restaurant. ■

LIGHTHOUSE TOURS

The Delaware Bay and Lighthouse Foundation offers boat rides across Lewes Harbor from May through September that take visitors into the interiors of the Delaware Breakwater East End Lighthouse and the Harbor of Refuge Lighthouse.

Harbor of Refuge stands sentinel at the mouth of the Bay. Its location is one of the most exposed on the eastern seaboard, described by the Foundation as "a place where mountainous seas pound the structure with walls of water that completely scale the beacon's towering stature." The Foundation opened the lighthouse to the public in 2003.

Light keepers resided in the Delaware Breakwater East End Lighthouse from 1885 until it was automated in 1950. Visitors can "imagine the feelings of isolation and loneliness of living in an offshore lighthouse, especially in wintertime when the nights are long."

Tours, limited to 24 or less passengers depending on the boat, leave from the Lewes-Cape Ferry terminal (subject to weather and the captain's judgment). Children must be at least 13 and meet a 46-inch height requirement. ∎

For a schedule of tour dates, check Delaware River & Bay Association at delawarebay-lights.org/ Tours.html

UNIVERSITY OF DELAWARE HUGH R. SHARP CAMPUS COLLEGE OF EARTH, OCEAN, AND ENVIRONMENT

A leading center of earth, ocean, and environmental science is located in Lewes at the campus of the University of Delaware, 700 Pilottown Road.   During the summer, knowledgeable guides give free tours of the facilities to the public.

Among the subjects discussed are environmental issues such as climate change, sea level rise, renewable energy, fish ecology, and harmful alga blooms. There are exhibits about scientific research on extreme environments like ice-covered Antarctic eco-systems and super-heated hydrothermal ocean vents.

Visitors see how researchers use satellites, surface monitors, and underwater robots to study oceans. They will also learn about the work of the College's fleet of research vessels, and the operations of the wind turbine.

Two aquariums display fish from local marine habitats. ■

Free tours of the facilities are given from June through August at 10:00 a.m. several days a week (for details and reservations call 302-645-4234, or e-mail dorey@udel.edu).

BLOCKHOUSE POND PARK

Blockhouse Pond Park is officially named George H.P. Smith Park, after Lewes' four-term African-American Mayor first elected in 1994. As a councilman in the 1980s, Smith cast the pivotal vote against constructing a major industrial coal-receiving port where the Cape Shores community now stands.

Blockhouse Pond Park offers a secluded oasis with a fenced children's playground, playing fields and a pond shaded with native flora and inhabited by indigenous fauna. This is a perfect place for a family picnic, especially with small children. The pond makes for good jogging, biking and even fishing.

Facilities include a butterfly garden, a walking path with benches and a horseshoe

pit. Grills and picnic tables are located near the island pavilion. ∎

Entrance at corner of Park Avenue and Johnson Street; parking off DuPont Avenue

DOWN ON THE FARM

Hopkins Farm Creamery/Green Acres Farm

Lewes-Georgetown Road and Dairy Farm Road (6 miles from St. Peter's Square, north on Route 9)

Hopkins Farm Creamery is an insider favorite for healthy-sized scoops of super-creamy ice cream. The Creamery is in the heart of Green Acres Farm (locally known as Hopkins Dairy), which is the largest dairy farm in the state of Delaware. So along with their peanut butter ripple or cappuccino delight cones, visitors get to see (and smell) the cows responsible for their ice cream.

Green Acres Farm has been owned and operated by the same family for four generations. The operation maintains over 1,000 head of cows (570 "milkers" and 500 replacement heifers). The Hopkins Henlopen Holsteins are milked three times a day, 365 days a year, producing some 12 million pounds of milk per year that is shipped immediately to Land O' Lakes agricultural cooperative for pasteurization, processing, packaging and distribution. The farm also works a thousand acres of corn, alfalfa, grass and small grain

Although visitors cannot tour the farm, for over twenty-five years Green Acres has opened its doors annually for two days to Sussex County 4-H agricultural education outreach for students in preschool to grade two. ∎

C&C ALPACA FACTORY

17219 Sweet Briar Road, Lewes 19958
(7 miles from St. Peter's Square, north
on Route 9)
609-752-7894

Alpacas are South America's domesticated version of the camel, prized for their lustrous, silky fleece long woven into textiles and ponchos by the people of the Andes.

C&C Alpaca Factory farm, on Sweetbriar Road seven miles from Lewes, raises a herd of thirty-some alpaca (along with a llama and two horses). The farm welcomes visitors, indeed encourages them to bring a box lunch to settle in and observe the gentle alpaca life style. "If you're having a really stressful day," says owner Chris Reachard, "you just come out and sit with the alpaca and feel your stress melt away."

There's an on-site store offering a wide range of alpaca yarns, scarves, hats, mittens and baby items. ■

LAVENDER FIELDS

18864 Cool Springs Road (7 miles from
St. Peter's Square, north on Route 9)
302-684-1514, 302-684-1602
www.lavenderfieldsde.com

Lavender Fields offers the feeling of Provence, France with its blooming rows of purple lavender, particularly at the peak of the season in July when the fragrance hangs heavy in the air. Delmarva proves to be ideally suited for the growth of these plants that thrive in sandy soil and welcome dry, sunny, windy locations.

Lavender is making a major resurgence as a modern herbal medicine, prized for its calming properties. It's used extensively in the manufacture of antiseptics, massage oils, and muscle soothers.

To say nothing of bubble baths and aromatherapy.

The five acre property with its Victorian farmhouse traces back to a deed from William Penn. Visitors can wander through the grounds picking their own bouquets, enjoying the scents, and luxuriating in the properties of these magical plants. They're free to walk the elaborate Labyrinth on the grounds, an exact duplicate of the one embedded in the floor of the famous Chartres (France) Cathedral that dates from the 13th century.

The ideal time to visit is July when the blooms are at the peak of their season and fragrance hangs heavy in the air.

The Cottage Store at the farm, open from 10:00 to 4:00, offers an array of lavender products for bath and body, sachets, and culinary purposes. ■

ANNUAL EVENTS

Lewes' calendar of annual events keeps growing. The full roster with dates and details can be found on the Events page at the Lewes Chamber of Commerce site: www.leweschamber.com/events/index

TULIP FESTIVAL

Lewes celebrates its Dutch heritage in glorious color with the flowering of thousands of tulips! Throughout the town's public parks is a spectacular display of a full array of varieties. Garden exhibits, workshops, and contests all weekend.

GARDEN TOUR

The annual Lewes Garden Tour at the end of June, a high point of the year, marks the unofficial kick-off to summer. Lewes is a town that prides itself on gardening and nowhere is that pride better showcased. Call it a variation of the Beatles' 'magical mystery tour' as visitors get to enter some half-dozen private gardens usually so sheltered from street-view that a passer-by would have no inkling of the wonder within.

The event began in 1990 when the late Mary Vessels, in whose honor Gazebo Square on Market Street is named, along with her brother and sister-in-law organized the first 'Zwaanendael

Heritage Garden Tour' to share the town's marvelous hidden gardens. "People walk by houses all the time in downtown Lewes," she observed, "and they would never know what wonderful Eden is there." The event's fame and popularity has steadily grown since then, the tour having been honored with a Governor's Tourism Award for Outstanding One Day Event.

The tour traditionally takes place the 3rd or 4th Saturday in June. Tickets can be bought in advance or on the day of the show at the visitor's center in the Fisher-Martin House, 120 Kings Highway. Refreshments are available at Zwaanendael Park and there is free shuttle service to the sites on the tour.

ST. PETER'S ART SHOW

On the first Saturday in July, from 9:00 a.m. to 4:00 p.m. Lewes becomes an art fair. While perhaps not quite in the same international collector's league as Art Basel or New York ArtExpo, the St. Peter's Art Show closes down St. Peter's Square and has become a bona fide Big Deal in Delmarva.

Upwards of 150 artists and artisans from throughout the east coast display their work, which has been an annual tradition since 1966 when it began as 'The Clothes Line Show'. Exhibits include paintings, sculptures, jewelry, ceramics, textiles, and photography.

The show is organized by St. Peter's Episcopal Church Women and raises funds for local charities. Food, featuring the ladies' now-famous Turkey Salad, is served in the parish hall. There is also a silent auction with donations from participating artists, as well as a raffle for the work of several featured artists.

Free parking with a shuttle to the Square is available at Shields Elementary School on Savannah Road. Parking is also usually available at Lewes Presbyterian Church (Kings Highway and Fourth Street), and Bethel United Methodist Church (Fourth and Market Streets).

FOURTH OF JULY

Lewes hosts an old-fashioned Fourth of July straight from the pages of Tom Sawyer. Second Street closes as the festivities begin with classic kids games (culminating with the ever-thrilling egg toss), and a blueberry pie-eating contest (in earlier days, the main event was a free-for-all up a greased pole where money awaited the first to the top, but too many injuries put an end to that).

In early afternoon, a processional of decorated boats wends down the Canal. Come five o'clock, the fabled 'Doo Dah' Parade weaves through town, a delightfully motley crew of serious (and less serious) tributes to patriotic pride (feel free to jump in and march along). It's Lewes' version of Mardi Gras!

Fireworks in the evening over Lewes Beach conclude the festivities with a bang!

ARTISTS' STUDIO TOUR

A number of regionally and nationally acclaimed artists call Lewes home. For the past 14 years, a group of them open their studios one Saturday for a public tour. The range of work differs depending on the artists but it is always diverse, from oil painting and fiber to textiles, jewelry and photography. For details and dates, check with Lewes Chamber of Commerce and www.LewesArt. Com

HOMETOWN CHRISTMAS PARADE, TREE LIGHTING AND CAROL SING

Another time-honored Lewes tradition and occasion for a parade with floats, marchers, cars and dogs! As the launch of the holiday season, this is a 'big deal' with winners awarded for such things as Most Original Entry, Classic Vehicles, and even Punkin Chunkin (categories are flexible, everybody gets at least Honorable Mention). Afterwards, there's the lighting of the town tree at Zwaanendael Park and festivities in the shops downtown.

LIVING LOCAL

LOCAL COORDINATES:

City of Lewes:
302-645-777, www.ci.lewes.de.us

Lewes Chamber of Commerce
and Visitors Bureau:
302-645-8073, www.leweschamber.com

Cape Henlopen State Park:
302-645-8983,
www.destateparks.com/park/cape-henlopen

Lewes Police Department:
911(Emergency);
(302)-645-6264 (non-emergency)

Lewes Historical Society:
(302)645-7670, www.historiclewes.org

Beebe Medical Center
424 Savannah Road
302-645-3300
Beebe Medical Center is a century-old 210 bed
not-for-profit community hospital that consistently ranks among winners of HealthGrade's
Distinguished Hospital Award for Clinical Ex-
cellence, rating in the top 5% of the nation's
hospitals in a variety of categories. It has also
been cited for providing high quality patient
care at an efficient cost.

'WHAT'S HAPPENING': BLOGS, TWEETS & SITES

Cape Gazette, the newspaper of record
on the Cape since its founding in 1993, posts a
daily up-date of the news and events on line.
capegazette.villagesoup.com

Lewes Chamber of Commerce
and Visitors Bureau posts a comprehensive list of local events that includes entertainment, theater, lectures, even zumba and
yoga. This is the place to start.
www.leweschamber.com/events

The Local Buzz:
A Community Newsletter
Deb Griffin keeps up with developments along
the Cape, especially new businesses, shops and
services with this knowledgeable free blog. To
subscribe, ping Deb at
debsmyagent@thedelawarebeaches.com

ActiveAdultsDelaware.com
An on-going gazette of news, events and community items published by real estate brokers
Kathy Sperl-Bell and Bill Bell.
lewes.activeadultsdelaware.com

LocalsOnlyBlog.com
This popular, underground guide to restaurant
specials at the beach and other insider deals is
published by Hadley McGregor.
www.localsonlyblog.com

GETTING HERE

Commercial Airports:
Philadelphia International Airport and Balti-
more-Washington International Airport (BWI)
are within two hours driving distance of Lewes.
Private airports: Georgetown (Del) Air Serv-
ices, Salisbury Regional Airport (Salisbury,
MD) is 45 miles away; New Castle Airport
(New Castle, DE) is 75 miles away.

Bus:
DC2NY Bus Company offers round-trip service to Rehoboth Beach (7.5 miles from Lewes)
from Washington (2 hours, 15 minutes), New
York (4 hours, 30 minutes), and Wilmington
(2 hours) during the summer. Days and times
change, so check for schedule details:
www.dc2ny.com

Train:
The closest train station is in Wilmington,
served by SEPTA Regional Rail services from
Philadelphia and Amtrak services.

THE LEWES BUSINESS SCENE CAN BEST BE DESCRIBED AS 'ECLECTIC'

People are always looking for 'the next destination' that they haven't heard of and they're finding Lewes. That is good for business. We're very fortunate to have the Ferry here; it introduces us to a steady flow of first-time visitors. Once people experience Lewes, they're drawn to its charms. It reminds them of the small town where they grew up or they compare it to Nantucket. They love the fact that once you park your car, you can wander around endlessly: visit museums, take a break for lunch, walk to the beach, have a drink on one of the porches.

What's really encouraging is that we're seeing a new generation of business owners in town, people in their thirties and forties who arrived in the last ten or fifteen years.

There's a wonderful assortment of restaurants that's drawing folks to town and they provide good synergy. More owners are keeping their shops open longer in-season to take advantage of Lewes as a food destination. We see it more every year, businesses extending their hours to offer visitors the chance to combine a shopping experience with their dining experience.

More and more people are living here year-round but Lewes is still seasonal. For some businesses, it's a challenge to deal with the seasonality. We're trying to keep people coming here on a more year-round basis with events like the Kite Festival on Good Friday, the Tulip Festival in April and the Maritime Festival in the fall. I've seen progress but the weather is the wild card.

When we have a banner weather year, the crowds are here. Ironically, good weather can sometimes work against the stores; people stay on the beach and don't go shopping. There's a real correlation between rainy days and higher sales volume." ∎

ACCOMODATIONS

Beacon Motel

514 East Savannah Road
302-645-4888
www.beaconmotel.com

The Beacon Hotel is located in downtown Lewes, on the 'beach' side across the draw-bridge from Second Street shopping and dining. 5 minute walk to Lewes Beach. Swimming pool and sundeck for guests. Adjoining the Lewes Cycle Shop (for bicycles), Beach Deli and Penninsula Art Gallery. Reasonably priced, clean, 'no frills'.

Black Hog Farmstead Bed & Breakfast

16371 New Road (Lewes)
302-236-2437, e-mail:
hwaite@gmail.com

Located minutes drive from downtown Lewes, one single guest suite with unparalleled privacy on acres of gardens and flowers (the owners are master gardeners), luxurious quiet nights and morning sunlight filtering through lace white curtains. Breakfast comes fresh to the table from the field. Pet-friendly, adults only.

Hotel Blue

110 Anglers Road
302-645-4880
www.hotelblue.info

Who would have ever predicted contemporary Euro-chic in Lewes and right on the canal! Besides huge flat-screens, the sixteen rooms and suites feature tile fire places, illuminated transparent sinks, and the hotel's signature color-changing ice bucket. Rooftop pool. Espresso machine in the front lobby. What's not to like?

Hotel Rodney

142 Second Street
302-645-6466
www.hotelrodneydelaware.com

Itself an historic gem (built in 1926), the Hotel Rodney is at the center of 'downtown' Lewes in St. Peter's Square. It combines B&B charm with New York boutique hotel sophistication. Twenty-four renovated and comfortable rooms, most of them on the 'small-ish' size. Property includes a workout facility. Popular Rose & Crown Pub adjoins the lobby.

Blue Water House

407 East Market Street
302-645-7832
www.lewes-beach.com

Very cool, laid-back B&B on the beach side of Lewes, two minute walk to the sand! Theme of this relaxed, inviting operation is Key West Casual. Colorful rooms with such names as 'Key Largo' and 'Key Lime' as well as 'The Hemingway Suite.' Were these the 'sixties,' Blue Water would be where the hippest of the hip hang out. Come to think of it, it still is!

Savannah Inn

330 Savannah Road
302-645-0330
www.savannahinnlewes.com

The Savannah Inn Bed and Breakfast offers luxurious accommodations in downtown, historic Lewes, Delaware, a short walk to shops and restaurants. The newly renovated turn of the century brick Victorian home boasts an updated, contemporary decor. B&B-types rank it among the best. "The room was spacious, the bathroom well appointed, the absolutely spotless house decorated with taste and simplicity," according to one guest.

The Inn at Canal Square
122 Market Street
302-644-3377
www.theinnatcanalsquare.com

'Nantucket' style boutique hotel, long the standard-setter for class amongst Lewes accommodations. 22 rooms and three suites, generously sized and tastefully appointed. Harborview rooms look out on the water. The Inn adjoins Canalfront Park and is in the midst of the historic district, making it an ideal location to experience the unique qualities of Lewes. Breakfast included.

The John Penrose Virden House
217 Second Street
302-644-0217
www.virdenhouse.com

An historic residence of one of Lewes' leading citizens, the Virden House is a tribute to the wonderful taste and gracious hospitality of its innkeepers (the multi-course breakfasts are legendary, served either in the dining room or on the spacious front porch overlooking St. Peter's Square). Extra-special is the York Cottage, behind the main house with its own private entrance in the lush garden. Five star ratings across the board.

Vesuvio Motel
105 Savannah Road
302-645-2224

Clean, simple, basic and well-loved by those who return year after year for its friendly atmosphere and welcoming owners. Located at the foot of the bridge to the beach side, it is in the midst of Second Street shopping and dining.

Beacon Mote

Blue Water House

Hotel Rodney

The Inn at Canal Square

Hotel Blue

ACKNOWLEDGEMENTS

Living Lewes is a project that I have wanted to do for a number of years. My wife Cait, son William, and I started coming here around 2005. Within several years, we were hooked and owners of a property on Mulberry Street, the get-away from our permanent home in D.C. I'm a journalist by temperament as well as profession; I like to know the 'back-story' of people and places. Lewes afforded me a perfect subject: small enough to 'grasp' in its entirety, complex enough to endlessly fascinate. Hence this book.

Many people have played vital roles in bringing Living Lewes to life. I approached Ted Becker and Mayor Jim Ford very early in the process, each offered encouraging support. A huge debt is owed Mike DiPaolo, Executive Director of the Lewes Historical Society, who is unfailingly generous with his time, astute with his knowledge, and inspiring in his enthusiasm. Thanks, too, to Jill DiPaolo who put the resources of wonderful Lewes Library (and particularly its Delaware Collection) at my disposal.

The spark of my high school compadre Rob Sturgeon and his partner Stephanie Bell ignited the project. They came to live here for a year from New York-ish gigs (she's a painter) and jumped into the writing and researching full throttle. Molly McMillan, local Sussex County girl and Cape Gazette journalist, brought her special blend of literary magic to the mix. Cari Flowers helped with design at critical moments. As a group, they make up 'The Mulberry Street Collective.'

A special thanks to Rob Waters, whose genius for design (and photography) breathes life into each page. Mark my words, this is one serious talent!

And, of course, the biggest thanks goes to Cait, who has been behind this project (and me) from the start, and to Will, who never wants to leave Lewes when it's time to return to reality.

Neil Shister

CPSIA information can be obtained
at www.ICGtesting.com
Printed in the USA
FSOW03n1836140617
35183FS